NEW PRACTICE READERS

second edition

Book C

DONALD G. ANDERSON
General Editor
Associate Superintendent, Retired
Oakland Public Schools
Oakland, California

CLARENCE R. STONE
with LINDA BARTON

Webster Division
McGraw-Hill Book Company

New York St. Louis San Francisco Auckland Bogotá Düsseldorf
Johannesburg London Madrid Mexico Montreal New Delhi
Panama Paris São Paulo Singapore Sydney Tokyo Toronto

New Practice Readers
Second Edition
Anderson

Project Editor: Carol Washburne
Editing Supervisor: Mary Naomi Russell
Design Supervisor: Margaret Amirassefi
Production Supervisor: Ellen B. Leventhal
Illustrators: William Harmuth, Phyllis Nathans, Tony Rao, Mike Sheean, Bill Shortridge
Cover and Text Design: Craven and Evans, Inc.

We wish to express our appreciation for permission to adapt and use copyrighted material as follows:

For "The Farmer's Helper" from "Rover, the Farmer's Helper" by Helen Fuller Orton, copyright 1924 by J. B. Lippincott Co., reprinted and adapted by permission.

For "A Clever Hunter" from "How an Indian Found His Game" by Mable Powers, copyright 1924 by J. B. Lippincott Co., reprinted and adapted by permission.

For "The Pie That Grew" from "The Thanksgiving Pie That Grew" by Carolyn Sherwin Bailey, reprinted and adapted by permission of Albert Whitman and Co., publishers.

Library of Congress Cataloging in Publication Data

Anderson, Donald George, date.
New practice readers.

Books B, F, and G by D. G. Anderson; Books C, D, and E by C. R. Stone, with L. Barton (Book C), A. Eliasberg (Book D), and E. Dolan (Book E).
1. Readers—1950– I. Burton, Ardis Edwards, joint author. II. Stone, Clarence R. III. Title.
PE1121.A56 1978 372.4'12 77-8845
ISBN 0-07-001902-9 (v. 1)

ISBN 0-07-001904-5

TO THE TEACHER

This book is one of a seven-book series. It is intended to provide reading interest along with comprehension skill development for readers who need additional practice material to achieve mastery. The controlled reading level of each book makes it possible to assign students to the text most suitable for individual reading comfort.

Readabilities for this book were confirmed with the Dale-Chall Readability Formula. The reading level should be comfortable for students whose reading skills are adequate for beginning fourth grade according to standardized tests.

This book contains nine groups of articles. The subjects cover major content fields. The pattern is as follows:

1. Progress
2. Early Americans
3. Pioneers
4. Insects and animals
5. Plant life
6. Courageous people
7. Arithmetic
8. American immigrants
9. Health and safety

Before each reading selection, there is a readiness activity to introduce difficult words. Teacher supervision at this point will be helpful to later success.

Following the articles, there are tests designed to improve specific skills for study reading. Charts at the end of this book provide a place for individual records of progress on each skill.

The six basic skills tested are consistent with those which appear on widely accepted reading achievement tests. In Book C, they are:

1. Finding specific answers and giving details. In questions of this type, particular words from the article must be used to complete the sentence. Students gain practice in remembering details.

2. Implied details. The answer here must be selected from among a group of possibilities. The correct answer is a reasonable conclusion (not one stated in the article) from ideas contained in the reading material. Answering and discussing such questions will give the student valuable experience in reasoning.

3. Meaning of the whole. These questions require that the student select the answer which best describes the central theme of the story.

4. Recognition of the correctness of a statement in relation to the selection. These questions give practice in verification of statements and develop increased precision in reading for meaning.

5. Awareness of the falseness of a statement in relation to the selection.

6. Recognition of the meanings of words in context.

At the conclusion of each unit of eight articles, there is a longer story prepared for recreational reading. Many of these stories come from folktales and are intended as pleasure reading and as a basis for group discussion. The *Thinking It Over* questions following each story may be used to launch the discussions or for written practice.

All the selections may be used to develop reading speed where desired. Students should be urged to increase their speed only in terms of their individual results.

A sample exercise precedes the regular lessons. Directions explain the procedure. Ideally, the teacher will work through the sample exercise with the group as a whole.

Read-along cassettes to help the most dependent students are available for Books A, B, C, and D.

TABLE OF CONTENTS

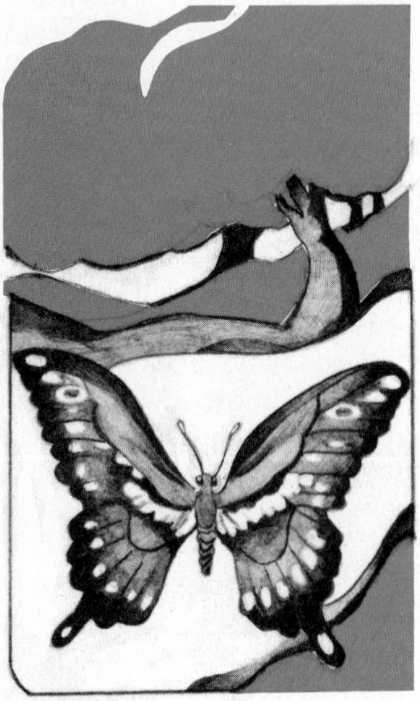

HOW TO USE THIS BOOK

There are three parts to each lesson.

1. Questions to help you get ready.
   Read them. Write the answers.

Getting Ready to Read

SAY AND KNOW

stroke
feeler
guard
important
juice
honeydew
herd
enemies
reason
collect
aphids
colony

Draw a line under the right answer or fill in the blank.

1. It means **the opposite of friends.** **guards** **enemies** **lice**
2. **To watch over** is **to** **stroke** **guard** **collect.**
3. **To rub gently** means **to** **guard** **collect** **stroke.**
4. If something means a lot to you, it is **important** **herd** **aphid.**
5. If something tells why, it is a **herd** **feeler** **reason.**
6. Another name for **plant lice** is ______________________.

---

2. A story to read.

Sample Tiny Cows

Most people know that farmers keep cows. But how many people know that ants also keep "cows"? The ants' "cows" are plant lice, called *aphids.* These are little insects that live on plants. Plant lice suck the juices from a plant until they are full.

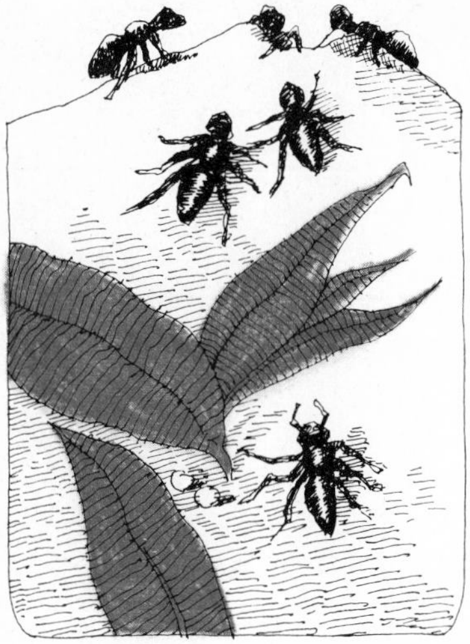

The aphids then make a juice, called *honeydew.* Ants eat the honeydew when it drops on plants. They also stroke the lice with their feelers to make more honeydew fall. It is for this reason that the lice are called "cows." The ants stroke the plant lice and eat the sweet juices.

The ants collect a herd of these "cows" and keep them near the ant colony. Here the lice eat green plants. The ants guard their "cows" from such insect enemies as the ladybug. Plant lice are important to ants, just as cows are important to farmers.

3. Questions to tell how well you read.
Read them. Write the answers.
Put the number right in the box.

Sample Testing Yourself **NUMBER RIGHT**

Draw a line under the right answer or fill in the blank.

1. Plant lice are the same to ants as ____________ are to farmers.

2. From the story, you can tell that
  a. ladybugs sometimes attack aphids.
  b. ants sometimes eat plant lice.
  c. plant lice eat only honeydew.

3. This story as a whole is about
  a. honeydew. c. ants.
  b. plants. d. ants' cows.

4. Farmers use plant lice as cows. Yes No Does not say

5. Aphids eat green plants. Yes No Does not say

6. What word in the first paragraph, fifth sentence, means **to draw up juice by the mouth?** ________________

Answers for Sample—Tiny Cows

Check your sample lesson. If you have made a mistake, correct it and decide why the given answer was right. Then record your score and begin your work in Book C.

Getting Ready to Read
1. enemies
2. guard
3. stroke
4. important
5. reason
6. aphids

Testing Yourself
1. cows
2. a
3. d√
4. Does not say
5. Does not say
6. such

Keeping Track of Your Progress

At the back of this book, on page 186, there are record charts. Turn to the charts and read the directions. After you finish each lesson, record your score. Keep track of how you are doing on each type of question.

If you may not mark in this book, make a copy of the charts for your notebook.

Book C NEW PRACTICE READERS

second edition

Getting Ready to Read

SAY AND KNOW

clever

bicycle

imagine

distances

travel

invention

motor

depend

Draw a line under the right answer or fill in the blank.

1. It means **to go places.** **imagine** **travel** **invention**
2. It is **an engine** or **a machine for moving things.** **clever** **travel** **motor**
3. **To picture in your mind** is to **imagine** **motor** **clever.**
4. **A two-wheeled thing to ride** is **a motor** **an invention** **a bicycle.**
5. **Something made from a new idea** is **a motor** **an invention** **travel.**
6. Someone with a sharp and active mind is ______________.

A-1 Wheels

How did anyone get the idea for the wheel? Did a log or a round rock rolling downhill set some clever person thinking? We can never know for sure. But we do know that people have come a long way by using the wheel.

Stop a minute. Think about all the things that you use every day that depend on wheels. Did

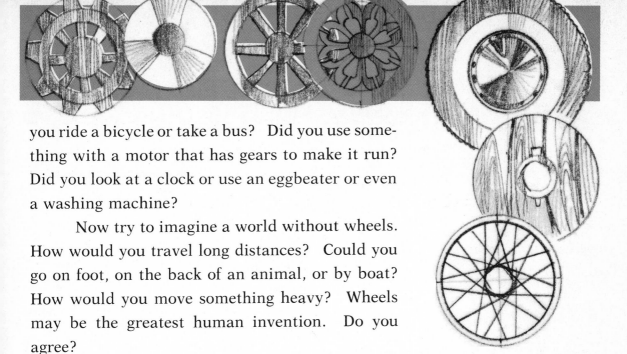

you ride a bicycle or take a bus? Did you use something with a motor that has gears to make it run? Did you look at a clock or use an eggbeater or even a washing machine?

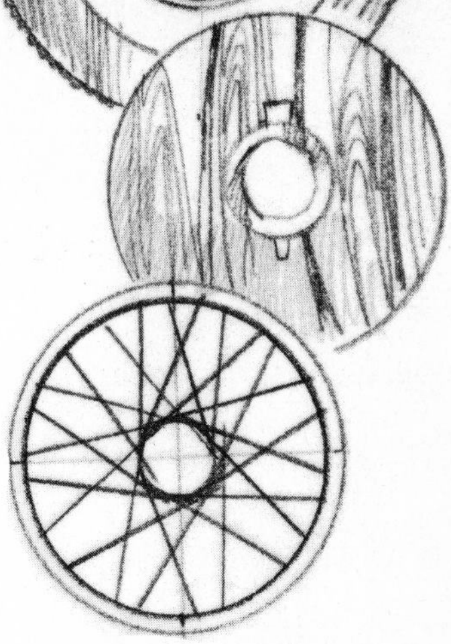

Now try to imagine a world without wheels. How would you travel long distances? Could you go on foot, on the back of an animal, or by boat? How would you move something heavy? Wheels may be the greatest human invention. Do you agree?

A-1 Testing Yourself

NUMBER RIGHT

Draw a line under the right answer or fill in the blank.

1. Today, many things have ____________________.

2. From the story, you can tell that

a. the wheel has been used as long as people have been on Earth.
b. we do not use the wheel for most things.
c. many people have found new uses for wheels.

3. This story as a whole is about

a. clocks with wheels.
b. traveling in the United States.
c. inventions of long ago.
d. wheels and their uses.

4. Some toys have wheels. Yes No Does not say

5. Motors have wheels. Yes No Does not say

6. What word in the second paragraph, second sentence, means **need** or **build upon?** ____________________

Getting Ready to Read

SAY AND KNOW

Missouri
Mandans
Sioux
Cheyenne
Pueblos
buffalo
plains
created
gather
different
peaceful
roamed
skilled
style
tribes
hunters

Draw a line under the right answer or fill in the blank.

1. **People who chase and kill animals for food** are **different** **hunters** **buffalo.**
2. **To collect something** is **to** **plant** **look** **gather.**
3. It means **not warlike.** **moving** **created** **peaceful**
4. It is a large animal. **plains** **buffalo** **style**
5. **To be good at doing something** is **to be** **skilled** **tribes** **style.**
6. It means **flat grasslands.** ____________________

A-2 The First Americans

In early America, many Native American tribes were very different from each other. The people from different places did not look the same. While most Native Americans had bronze-colored skin and dark hair, some did not. The Mandans from the Missouri Valley had light skin and hair.

The tribes were also different in the way they lived. Many tribes got their food by gathering plants and by hunting. These people usually stayed in one area. In contrast, the Sioux and the Cheyenne were buffalo hunters who roamed the plains. Even before they had horses, the Sioux and the Cheyenne traveled a great deal from place to place.

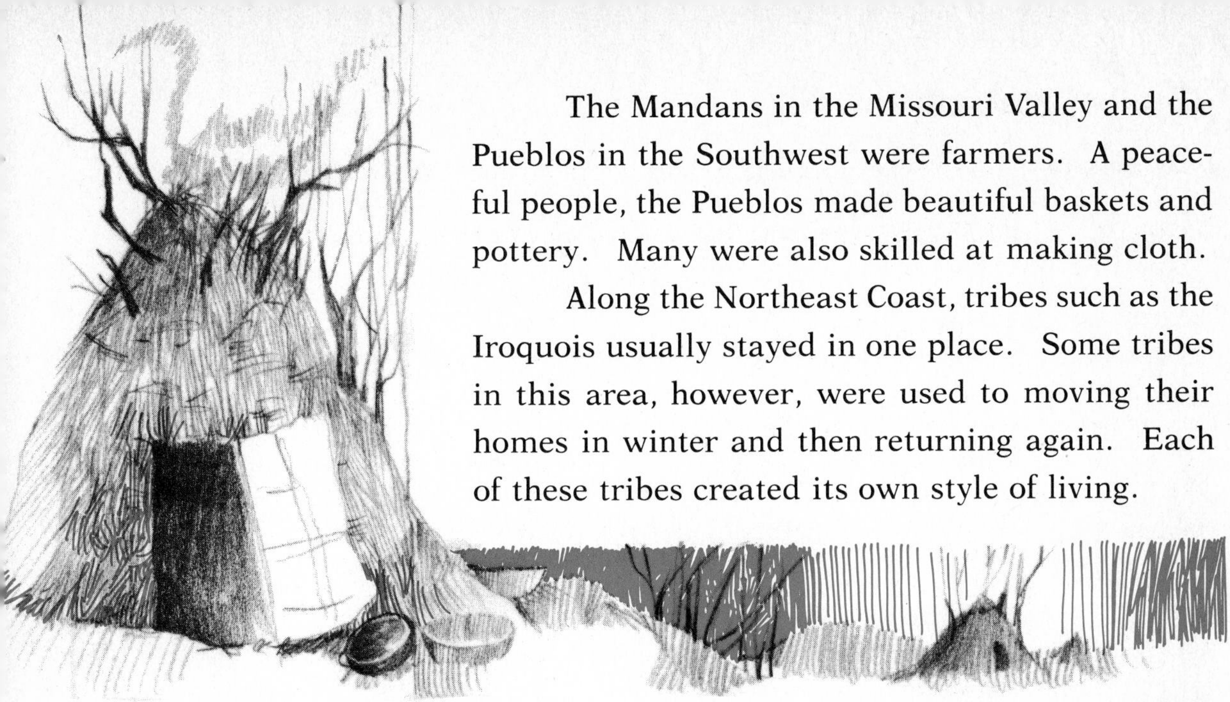

The Mandans in the Missouri Valley and the Pueblos in the Southwest were farmers. A peaceful people, the Pueblos made beautiful baskets and pottery. Many were also skilled at making cloth.

Along the Northeast Coast, tribes such as the Iroquois usually stayed in one place. Some tribes in this area, however, were used to moving their homes in winter and then returning again. Each of these tribes created its own style of living.

A-2 Testing Yourself

NUMBER RIGHT ______

Draw a line under the right answer or fill in the blank.

1. The Sioux and the Cheyenne roamed the ______________________.

2. From the story, you can tell that
   a. not all Native Americans led the same kind of life.
   b. Native Americans in the Southwest roamed the plains.
   c. Native Americans were not afraid of horses.

3. This story as a whole is about
   a. Native American styles of living.
   b. Native Americans of the East.
   c. the coming of the buffalo.
   d. what Native Americans ate.

4. The Sioux and the Cheyenne were buffalo hunters.
Yes No Does not say

5. The Mandans had dark hair. Yes No Does not say

6. What word in the last sentence means about the same as **made?**

____

Getting Ready to Read

SAY AND KNOW

cozy
coast
covered
oxen
tools
trail
farther
mobile
barrel
settle

Draw a line under the right answer or fill in the blank.

1. Something that has a top is **cozy mobile covered.**
2. If it can be moved, it is **coast mobile farther.**
3. **To set up a new home** means **to settle trail coast.**
4. It means about the same as **path. trail barrel oxen**
5. It is **the part of the land that meets the sea.**
   trail oxen coast
6. **Things to work with** are called ___________.

A-3 The First Mobile Homes

Mobile homes today give people a cozy space to live in. If they choose, they can move their homes when they need to. In a way, early European settlers in North America had mobile homes, too.

At first, many Spanish people settled in California and in the Southwest. Many English families settled along the East Coast. In time, they needed more room and new lands. In the 1800s, the people on the East Coast began to move farther west.

The families put everything they could carry into covered wagons pulled by teams of oxen. Pioneers took food, clothing, and kitchen tools. Often they took furniture and farming tools. They

sometimes took their pets, one or more cows, sheep, and horses. They traveled over bad roads that were just trails with ruts made by other wagons.

One woman told about such a trip that her ancestors had made. She said that her grandmother milked the cows in the morning. Then the milk was put into a barrel. The ride was so bumpy that by night they had butter!

A-3 Testing Yourself

NUMBER RIGHT

Draw a line under the right answer or fill in the blank.

1. In a way, European settlers had ________________ homes.

2. From the story, you can tell that
- a. people did not move west in America before 1800.
- b. people went west looking for gold.
- c. people going west took everything they could with them.

3. This story as a whole is about
- a. modern travel.
- b. living on the East Coast.
- c. moving west in the early days.
- d. Native Americans in America.

4. Travel by covered wagon was bumpy. Yes No Does not say

5. Everyone traveled east in the 1800s. Yes No Does not say

6. What word in the last sentence means about the same as **rough?**

____

Getting Ready to Read

SAY AND KNOW

silk
silkworm
nature
surprise
cocoon
moth
mulberry
hatch
Chinese
unwind

Draw a line under the right answer or fill in the blank.

1. It is **a tree.** **silk** **cocoon** **mulberry**
2. One kind of fine cloth is called **silk** **moth** **Chinese.**
3. **Something unexpected** is **a** **moth** **nature** **surprise.**
4. It is **an insect.** **moth** **hatch** **silk**
5. Things like birds, insects, and trees are part of **nature** **silk** **surprises.**
6. It means **the opposite of wind.** ______

A-4 A House of Silk

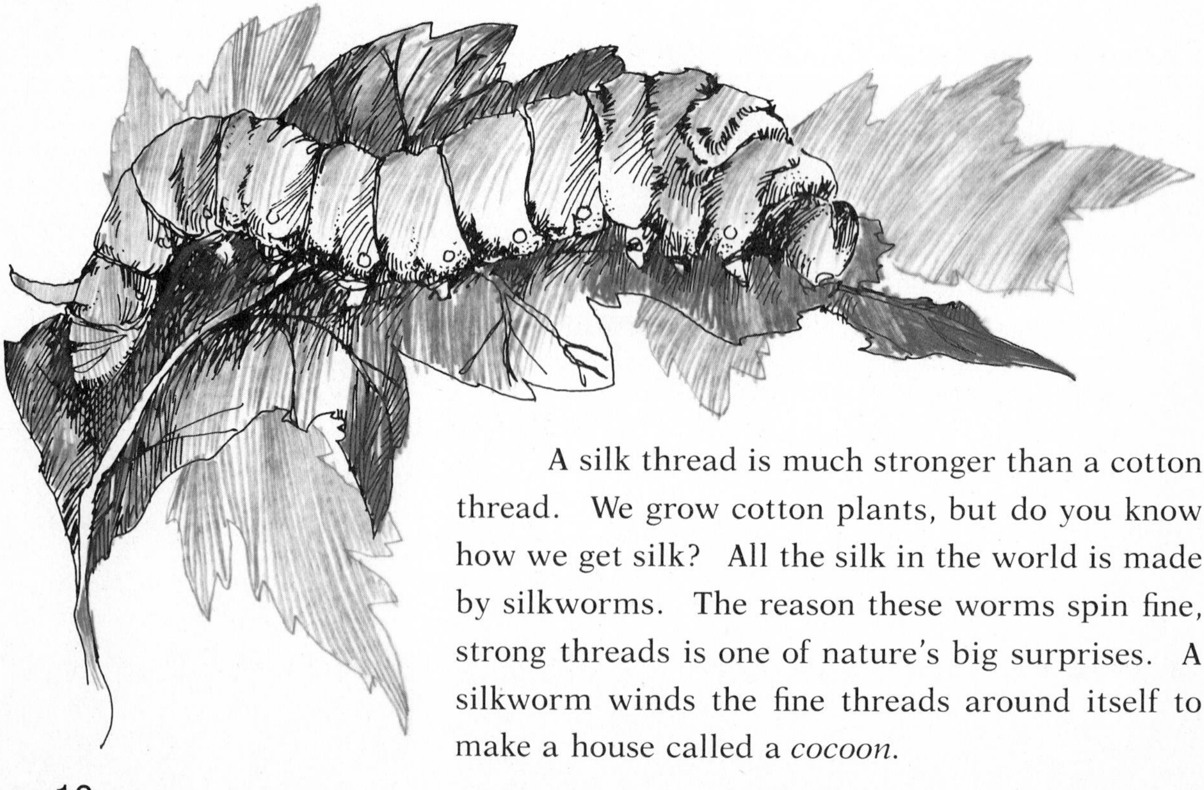

A silk thread is much stronger than a cotton thread. We grow cotton plants, but do you know how we get silk? All the silk in the world is made by silkworms. The reason these worms spin fine, strong threads is one of nature's big surprises. A silkworm winds the fine threads around itself to make a house called a *cocoon*.

A silkworm lives inside its cocoon for two or three weeks. During the time it lives in the cocoon, it changes from a worm to a moth. The moth comes out slowly, pushing a hole in one end of the cocoon. Soon the moth's wings open, and off it flies.

Then the moth lays eggs on the leaves of a mulberry tree. From these eggs, tiny worms hatch. They grow big on the food that is near. Finally, each one of the new worms spins a silk thread and winds it into a cocoon of its own.

The Chinese were the first people to unwind the cocoon and to use the silk thread. It is still used today in fine clothing.

A-4 Testing Yourself

NUMBER RIGHT

Draw a line under the right answer or fill in the blank.

1. A cocoon is a silkworm's ____________.

2. From the story, you can tell that
   a. people can make silk.
   b. the Japanese were the first people to use silk.
   c. without silkworms, we would have no silk.

3. This story as a whole is about
   a. the Chinese people.
   b. silkworms and silk.
   c. mulberry trees.
   d. growing cotton.

4. Native Americans raised silkworms. Yes No Does not say

5. Silkworms turn into moths. Yes No Does not say

6. What word in the second sentence means about the same as **raise?**

____

Getting Ready to Read

SAY AND KNOW

pitcher
pitcherlike
strange
growths
purple
brighter
trap
sticky
unable

Draw a line under the right answer or fill in the blank.

1. You can get caught in it. **growth** **shape** **trap**
2. It is a color. **pitcher** **purple** **strange**
3. It means about the same as **odd.** **trap** **unable** **strange**
4. **Something used to carry water** is a **shape** **trap** **pitcher.**
5. If it is like glue, it is **brighter** **sticky** **strange.**
6. It means **more bright.** ____________________

A-5 An Unhappy Slide

Have you ever heard of plants that eat insects? That may sound strange, but there are plants that really use flies and bugs for food.

One of these is the pitcher plant. Some pitcher plants have leaves that are pitcher-shaped. Others have pitcherlike growths at the ends of their leaves. One pitcher is green with spots of purple. The lip and mouth of the pitcher are brighter in color than the other parts.

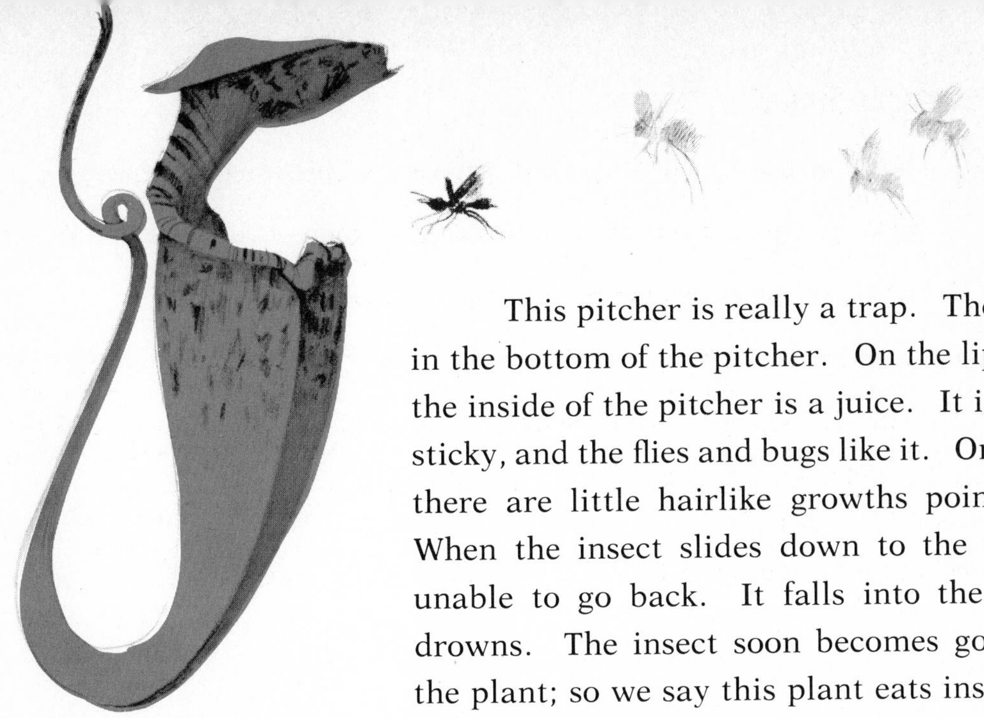

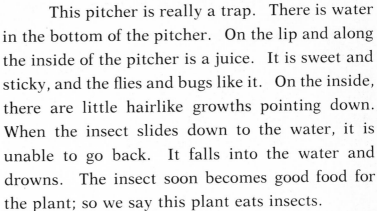

This pitcher is really a trap. There is water in the bottom of the pitcher. On the lip and along the inside of the pitcher is a juice. It is sweet and sticky, and the flies and bugs like it. On the inside, there are little hairlike growths pointing down. When the insect slides down to the water, it is unable to go back. It falls into the water and drowns. The insect soon becomes good food for the plant; so we say this plant eats insects.

A-5 Testing Yourself

NUMBER RIGHT

Draw a line under the right answer or fill in the blank.

1. Insects are food for some ________________________.

2. From the story, you can tell that
- a. insects do not know that some plants are traps.
- b. some bugs eat plants because they are sticky.
- c. all insects drink water from plants.

3. This story as a whole is about
- a. flies and bugs.
- b. insects.
- c. pitcher plants trapping insects.
- d. plants that are green.

4. Some plants eat other plants. Yes No Does not say

5. Insects can swim. Yes No Does not say

6. What word in paragraph two, sentence three, means **things growing on something?** ____________________

Getting Ready to Read

SAY AND KNOW	Draw a line under the right answer or fill in the blank.
college	**1.** It is **a school for older students.** **college** **lessons** **law**
language	**2.** It means **words that are written or spoken.** **language** **private** **workers**
strange	
laws	**3.** Something that is just for a few people is called **lessons** **private** **laws.**
private	
lessons	**4.** **The opposite of familiar** is **private** **lessons** **strange.**
grown	**5.** If you are no longer a child, you are **grown** **fair** **strange.**
successful	**6.** A lawyer is someone who studies ________.

A-6 She Knew What She Wanted

Belva Lockwood's family thought she wanted strange things. She was a grown woman with a child. And she still wanted to go to college! Her sister was so upset by such ideas that she started to cry. Women in the 1800s were not supposed even to think of going to college. But Belva Lockwood had made up her mind. She knew what she wanted.

Years later, Lockwood was working for the rights of women workers. She couldn't understand the language of the laws. Again, she made up her mind. She must go to law school.

Time after time, law schools said *No!* No women had gone there before. None could come in now.

Finally, Lockwood worked out a plan. She got the head of one law school to give her private lessons. Belva Lockwood did become a lawyer, and a successful one. She changed laws for women, for blacks, and for Native Americans. She never stopped trying to make things fair. In 1884, she even ran for President of the United States.

A-6 Testing Yourself

NUMBER RIGHT

Draw a line under the right answer or fill in the blank.

1. Young Lockwood found that she couldn't understand the language of the ____________.

2. From the story, you can tell that
   a. Lockwood's sister also went to college to study law.
   b. most women in the 1900s are lawyers.
   c. Lockwood helped both white and black women.

3. This story as a whole is about
   a. a successful doctor.
   b. a successful lawyer.
   c. going to college.
   d. American presidents.

4. Lockwood was a lawyer for ten years. Yes No Does not say

5. Lockwood knew what she wanted to do. Yes No Does not say

6. What word in the first sentence means about the same as **unusual?**

____

Getting Ready to Read

SAY AND KNOW

equator
diameter
Challenger
Amazon
Mississippi
Missouri
Illinois
Arkansas
drainage
basin
geography
encyclopedia
amazing

Draw a line under the right answer or fill in the blank.

1. **A set of books that contains facts about almost everything** is
   an encyclopedia a basin a diameter.
2. Something that causes wonder is
   a basin amazing a diameter.
3. **A bowl or an area of land drained by a set of rivers** is
   an equator a basin geography.
4. **A straight line through the center of a sphere or a ball** is its
   equator basin diameter.
5. **The imaginary dividing line between the north and south ends of the Earth** is **a diameter the equator a basin.**
6. **The study of the Earth** is ____________________.

A-7 The Big Numbers of the Earth

It's fun to know the great big numbers of the highest and the deepest and the longest places on Earth. For example, the Earth itself measures 40,075.16 kilometers (24,901.55 miles) around the equator. The diameter, or distance through the Earth at its center, is 12,756.32 kilometers (7926.41 miles). The highest mountain in the world, Mt. Everest, is 8848 meters (29,028 feet) above sea level. The deepest place that we know of in the oceans is the Challenger Deep near Guam. It is 11,033 kilometers (36,198 feet) deep.

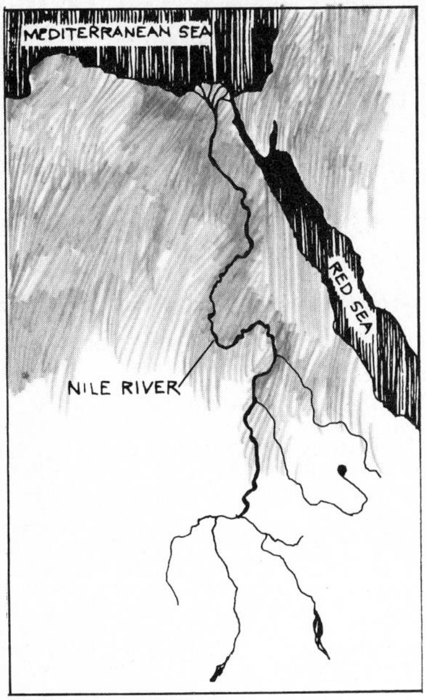

The longest river in the world is the Nile. It is 6738 kilometers (4187 miles) long. The Amazon River in South America is the second longest. Its length is 6437 kilometers (4000 miles). In the United States, the longest river is the Mississippi, which is 4241 kilometers (2635 miles) in length. The Missouri, the Illinois, the Arkansas, and other rivers that connect with the Mississippi, have a drainage basin that is 3,230,490 square kilometers (1,241,300 square miles) in size.

Your geometry book and the encyclopedia are full of these amazing numbers. Can you find the five longest rivers in the world?

A-7 Testing Yourself

NUMBER RIGHT

Draw a line under the right answer or fill in the blank.

1. Facts about mountains may be found in ______________ books.

2. From the story, you can tell that
   a. people have learned a lot about the Earth.
   b. geography and history are the same.
   c. the Arkansas River is the longest in the United States.

3. This story as a whole is about
   a. geography facts.
   b. the tallest mountains.
   c. rivers that flow to the sea.
   d. long rivers that cause floods.

4. The United States has many long rivers. Yes No Does not say

5. Big numbers are often found in small books. Yes No Does not say

6. What word in the second paragraph, last sentence, means about the same as **join together?** ______________

Getting Ready to Read

SAY AND KNOW

newcomers
pave
continue
continued
starve
foreigners
style
America
United States

Draw a line under the right answer or fill in the blank.

1. Thousands of newcomers arrived in the **United States** **house** **streets.**
2. **To cover streets with something** is to **starve** **pave** **jet.**
3. **To die from lack of food** is to **pray** **style** **starve.**
4. It means **keep going.** **arrive** **make** **continue**
5. **People who are new to a place** are **many** **strange** **newcomers.**
6. It is another name for the United States. ____________

A-8 A New Home for Many

In the 1800s and early 1900s, the United States welcomed thousands of newcomers. In their homes across the sea, many were not allowed to live or pray as they wished. They were poor. Many were almost starving. The immigrants came here looking for a life of freedom. Some even said that in America the streets would be paved with gold.

When they arrived, the immigrants looked strange to Americans. They were dressed in the style of their homelands. That seemed odd. They spoke their own languages. That seemed strange to many people here, too. Slowly, those newcomers made a fresh start in life. They became Americans instead of "foreigners."

In recent years, people have continued to come to America in hopes of a better life. But today, many arrive by jet plane. Some want to become doctors. Others want to be in sports or to run their own businesses. They want to be in a country where they will feel free to do these things.

A-8 Testing Yourself

NUMBER RIGHT

Draw a line under the right answer or fill in the blank.

1. Some immigrants thought they would find streets paved with ____________.

2. From the story, you can tell that
   a. immigrants usually have much to learn about their new country.
   b. immigrants almost never learn English.
   c. immigrants always like all the new ways of life they find.

3. This story as a whole is about
   a. how to fly a jet plane.
   b. immigrants in the United States.
   c. how to dig for gold.
   d. people who like to travel.

4. People still come to the United States to find a better life.
   Yes   No   Does not say

5. Many newcomers arrive by jet plane.   Yes   No   Does not say

6. What word in the second paragraph, last sentence, means **people from outside one's own country?** ____________

Getting Ready to Read

SAY AND KNOW

alley
team
proud
ashamed
trash
weeds
apartment
neighborhood
pleasant

Draw a line under the right answer or fill in the blank.

1. It means **a narrow path between or behind buildings.**
   alley **weeds** **team**
2. **Things that are thrown away** are **trash** **pleasant** **alley.**
3. It means **wild plants.** **alley** **weeds** **apartment**
4. If you are pleased with your work, you are
   team **ashamed** **proud.**
5. It means **feeling bad about doing wrong.**
   ashamed **proud** **alley**
6. It means the same as **a group.** ____________________

A-9 A Big Cleanup

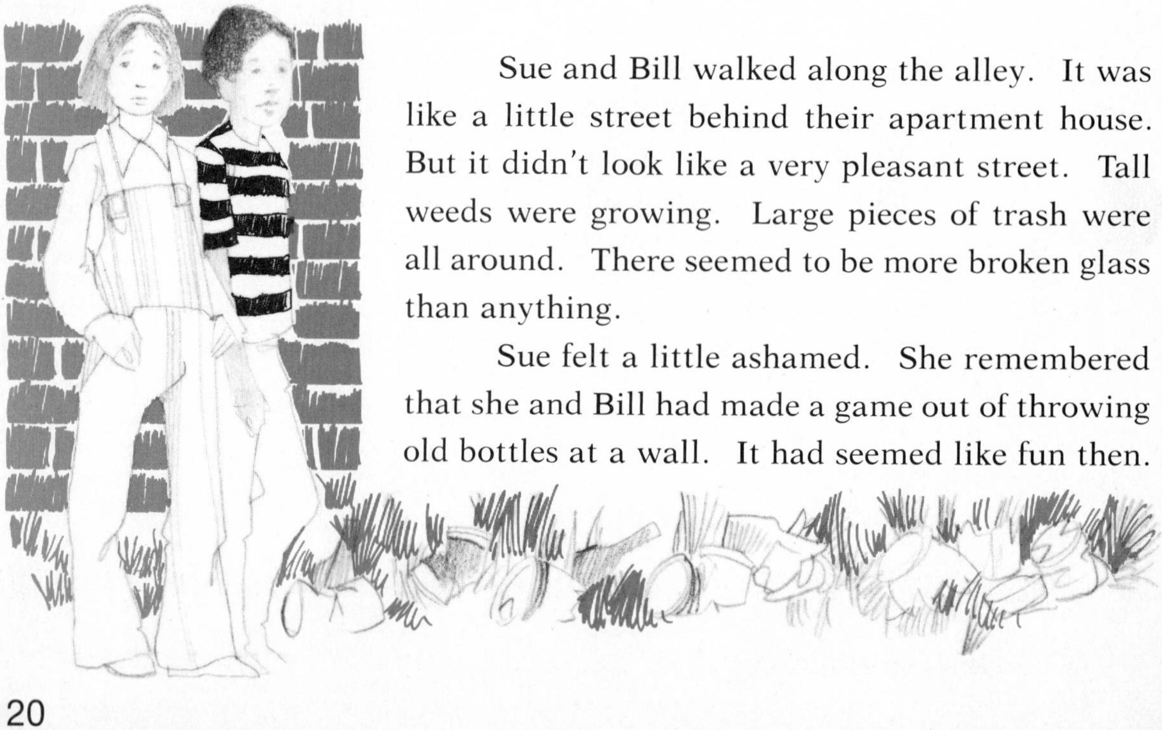

Sue and Bill walked along the alley. It was like a little street behind their apartment house. But it didn't look like a very pleasant street. Tall weeds were growing. Large pieces of trash were all around. There seemed to be more broken glass than anything.

Sue felt a little ashamed. She remembered that she and Bill had made a game out of throwing old bottles at a wall. It had seemed like fun then.

But looking at the mess, she wasn't feeling very happy.

"Bill," she said, "we'd better make a change here. Let's call that neighborhood group together this afternoon to make plans."

The next Saturday, some changes were made. Sue, Bill, and a group of friends formed a team. Their job was to go through the alleys behind their apartment houses. They swept up the glass. Neighbors helped get a truck that took away the trash. When the job was done, Sue and Bill were proud of their team. They made plans to work every month.

A-9 Testing Yourself

NUMBER RIGHT

Draw a line under the right answer or fill in the blank.

1. The alley was like a little ______________________.

2. From the story, you can tell that
   a. most people want to help each other improve things.
   b. no one would help Sue with her neighborhood plans.
   c. Sue and Bill only wanted to be team leaders.

3. This story as a whole is about
   a. finding ways to improve things.
   b. Bill's and Sue's school.
   c. careless children.
   d. breaking old bottles.

4. Broken glass helped make a mess. Yes No Does not say

5. Sue liked to work on Saturdays. Yes No Does not say

6. What word in the last paragraph, second sentence, means the same as **got together** or **made?** ______________________

Justice for a Horse

Long ago, in a little town called Atri, there lived a wise ruler. So that all might have justice, the ruler hung a big bell in the market place. A long rope was tied to it. Then the royal messenger called out this news:

"Hear ye! Hear ye! Anyone may ring this bell and ask for justice. When you ring the bell, the judges will come to hear your case and see that justice is done!"

Over the years, the bell was rung many times.

In the course of time, the rope grew frayed and old. It got shorter and shorter. Finally, it was too short for a child to reach.

"Order a new rope," said the ruler.

"I have a vine," one person said. "It will do until the new rope comes." She tied the vine to the old rope. There it hung, once again within easy reach for all the people.

In the hills near Atri, there lived a rich old knight. He had been a brave soldier in his time. He had ridden a fine horse. More than once, this horse had saved the

knight's life. The two had been real friends. As the knight grew old, he changed. His love of gold grew and grew. Nothing in the world was as important to him as bags of money. One morning, he looked out his window and saw the old horse. "How foolish it is to feed that old horse now," he cried. "It is no longer of use to me. Turn it out."

Down the road walked the old horse. It was half blind and nearly starved. The horse wandered into the market place of Atri early in the afternoon. All the people of Atri were asleep, as they always were during this hot part of the day. The

hungry horse saw the vine. It reached for a green leaf.

"Dong!" sounded the bell. The old horse jumped, but it reached for more leaves. As it tugged at them, the bell sounded a clear call again and again. The judges woke. At once, they put on their robes and came to give justice. Many people also came. Everyone pitied the horse.

"Send for the knight," cried the judges.

When the knight came, he hung his head and said nothing.

"You will care for this horse as long as it lives," said the judges. The people cheered.

"Our ruler is wise," said one. "Who would think that the bell of Atri could bring justice even to an old horse?"

MY READING TIME ______ (410 WORDS)

Thinking It Over

1. Did the people of Atri think the horse had rung the bell on purpose?
2. What are some of the countries where the people nap during the hot part of the day?
3. Can you think of a reason why the ruler's plan for justice might not always work?

Getting Ready to Read

SAY AND KNOW	
	Draw a line under the right answer or fill in the blank.
cause	**1.** It is **a grain from which bread is made.** **wheat** **crops** **tractor**
wheat	
machinery	**2. Picking crops that are ripe** is **pollution** **wheat** **harvesting.**
harvests	**3.** It is **a farm machine.** **crops** **automobile** **tractor**
harvesting	**4. Plants grown for food** are **pollution** **crops** **tractors.**
crops	**5.** It means **making things dirty.**
pollution	**pollution** **machine** **harvesting**
tractor	**6.** What word means **to make happen?** ________________

B-1 Using Machines

Long, long ago, people had only their own hands and very simple tools for making things. Today, we have hundreds of machines to help us.

Once, people used only animals to pull carts or wagons. Today, engines do most of our pulling. Our lives are full of the roar of automobile engines, lawnmowers, airplanes, and powerboats.

In the past, people did their planting by hand. Wheat, cotton, corn, and other seeds were planted with plain hand tools. Today, machinery is used to plant and harvest the crops. The farm tractor is run by an engine. So are the corn picker, the cotton picker, and the cherry-harvesting machine.

Today, machines make it possible to have good roads and smooth streets. We have machines for making our tools, as well as machines to move dirt and rocks from one place to another.

Our new machines sometimes cause new problems of pollution. It seems that all new things have a good side and a bad side.

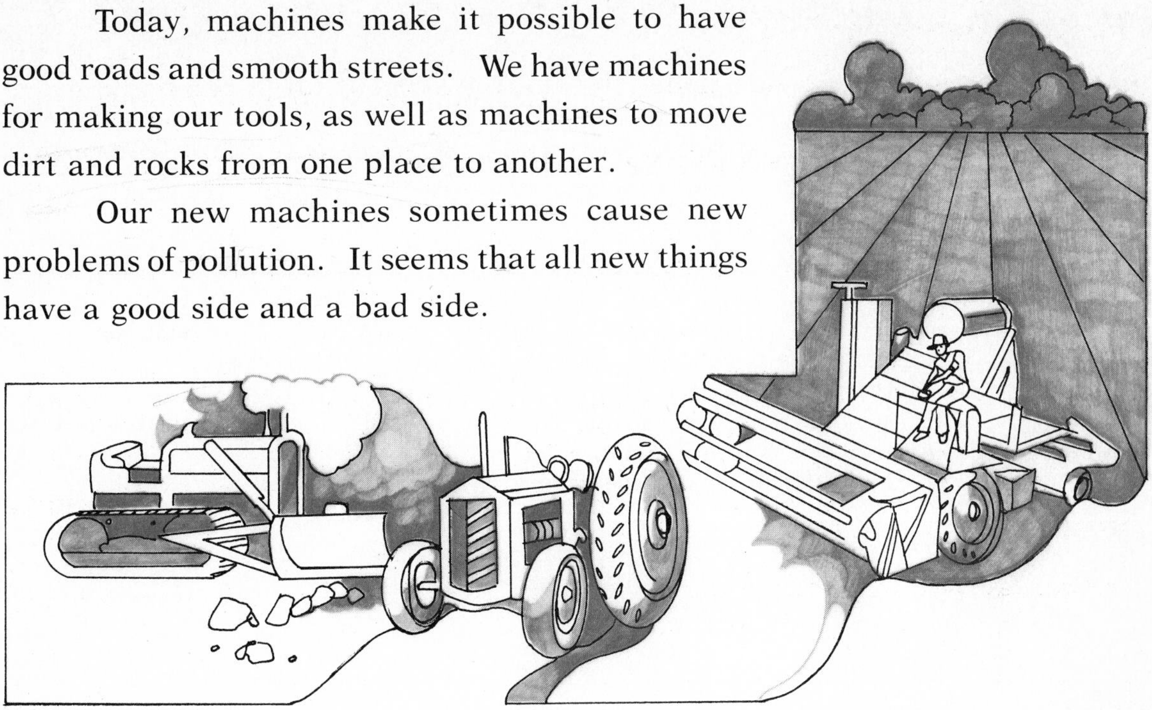

B-1 Testing Yourself

NUMBER RIGHT

Draw a line under the right answer or fill in the blank.

1. Machines sometimes cause problems of ____________________.

2. From the story, you can tell that
- a. machines have helped us to live better.
- b. machines are not good.
- c. machine-made products are better than handmade things.

3. This story as a whole is about
- a. working on farms.
- b. making engines.
- c. building roads.
- d. helpful machines.

4. Some crops are planted by machine. Yes No Does not say

5. Good streets and roads cost a lot. Yes No Does not say

6. What word in the second sentence means **aid?** ____________

Getting Ready to Read

SAY AND KNOW	Draw a line under the right answer or fill in the blank.
expert	1. It means **someone who knows a great deal about something.** **adobe expert group**
slant	2. Something on an angle rather than straight is on a **slant plank shelter.**
shelter	3. It means **a board. plank slant shelter**
plank	4. It is the same as **a safe place. adobe apartment shelter**
adobe	5. **Something that supports a house** is called **a tribe frame large.**
frame	
miniature	6. It means **something very small.** ________________

B-2 Many Houses

Not all Native Americans built the same kinds of houses. The tribes of the Northwest Coast lived in slant-roofed houses built of cedar planks. These shelters were 9 by 12 meters (about 30 feet by 40 feet). They stood nearly 2 to 3 meters (6 to 10 feet) high.

The large houses of the Iroquois, called *longhouses,* might be as long as 45 meters (150 feet). Many members of the same family shared the house. They built the house large enough so that no one would be left out.

Some California tribes lived in simple, earth-covered or brush shelters. Other Native Americans in this area had redwood plank houses. In the

Southwest, some farming tribes built pueblos. They were large, tall houses of stone and adobe that looked like apartment houses.

Usually, the women of the Great Lakes built the wigwams. Little girls practiced by making miniature wigwams for their dolls. Since many tribes often moved their villages, the women were also expert movers. Many times, they carried their belongings from place to place on their backs. When they moved, they left nothing behind. Those who lived in wood houses left only the frames behind.

B-2 Testing Yourself

NUMBER RIGHT

Draw a line under the right answer or fill in the blank.

1. Usually, women built the ____________________.
2. From the story, you can tell that
   a. the people of a single tribe built the same kind of house.
   b. Native Americans always used stone to build their houses.
   c. Native Americans usually lived in caves.
3. This story as a whole is about
   a. Native Americans of the Southwest.
   b. adobe houses and brush shelters.
   c. Native American houses.
   d. the Plains people.
4. Tribes on the St. Lawrence River were warlike. Yes No Does not say
5. Longhouses were very hard to build. Yes No Does not say
6. What word in the third paragraph, last sentence, means **sun-dried brick made of clay?** ____________

Getting Ready to Read

SAY AND KNOW	Draw a line under the right answer or fill in the blank.
game	**1. Someone who settles in the wilderness** is a
sod	____________________.
settle	2. One kind of bird often hunted for food is **a sod quail fish.**
wilderness	**3. Land with wild animals and plants and no people** is a **well market wilderness.**
pioneer	**4.** It means **a spread of land. area quail game**
quail	**5.** It means **to make a home in a place. sod settle area**
squirrels	**6.** It means **wild animals, fish, or birds that are hunted.**
area	____________

B-3 Where to Settle

Pioneers who moved to new lands carefully chose a place to go. Some families looked for rich land to farm. Others wanted to find wild animals that had fur. A good living could be made by catching these animals and selling the fur. Some traders made their living by buying these furs and taking them to market. Often, too many animals were killed. Many hunters and traders then decided to move on to find more.

Pioneers liked to settle where there was plenty of wild game for food. Deer, quail, geese, turkeys, ducks, squirrels, and rabbits made good

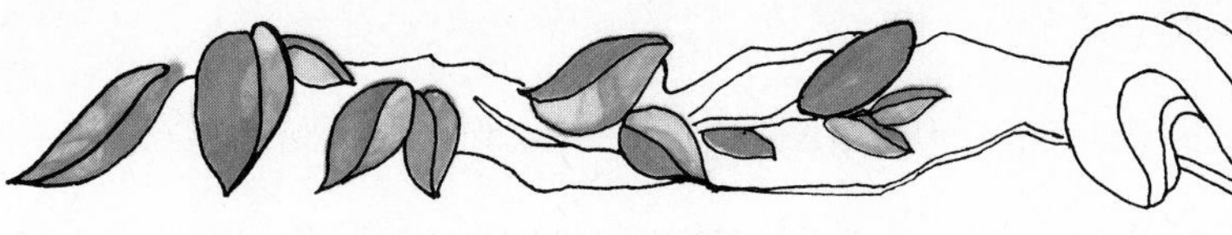

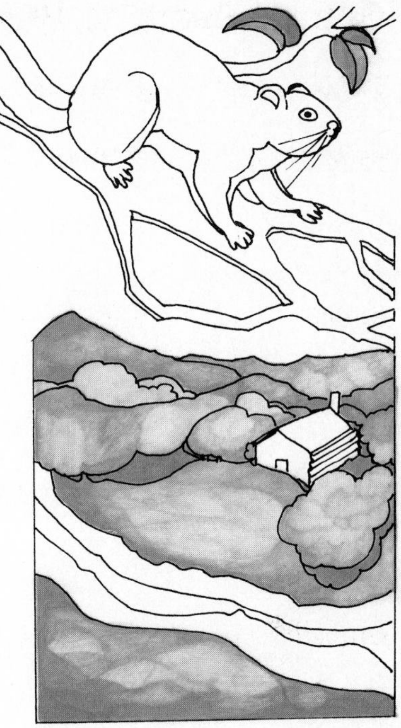

food. Pioneers sometimes settled where plenty of fish could be caught.

Pioneers liked to build their houses in places where they could get good water by drinking from a spring or by digging a well. Many houses were made of squares of earth and grass called *sod*. People who wanted to build houses made of logs liked to settle near a place with trees. In this wilderness, sometimes only one family settled in an area. Its members had to travel miles and miles to see another family.

B-3 Testing Yourself

NUMBER RIGHT

Draw a line under the right answer or fill in the blank.

1. Often, too many animals were ______________________.

2. From the story, you can tell that
   a. pioneers thought carefully about where to settle.
   b. all pioneers were farmers or trappers.
   c. the government chose places for pioneers to settle.

3. This story as a whole is about
   a. lands west of the Rockies.
   b. frontier life.
   c. fur trading on the Mississippi.
   d. pioneers choosing places to settle.

4. Pioneers liked wild game. Yes No Does not say

5. Many families always lived together. Yes No Does not say

6. What word in the first sentence means **with care?** ______________________

Getting Ready to Read

SAY AND KNOW

butterfly
caterpillar
weather
burst
weak
sail
underneath
underside
attached

Draw a line under the right answer or fill in the blank.

1. It means **to break open.** **burst** **weak** **sail**
2. **Joined to** means **underneath** **attached** **burst.**
3. It means **the opposite of strong.** **weak** **sail** **burst**
4. It means **the opposite of top.** **weak** **burst** **underside**
5. It is another way of saying **to fly.** **sail** **attach** **caterpillar**
6. A caterpillar, which is like a worm, changes into a beautiful

______________________.

B-4 One of Nature's Wonders

We do not really understand how a caterpillar can change into a different insect. But we do know that the fat caterpillar grows from a tiny egg laid by a butterfly on the underside of a leaf.

This caterpillar climbs up the stem of a plant. It spins a tiny silk thread and makes a kind

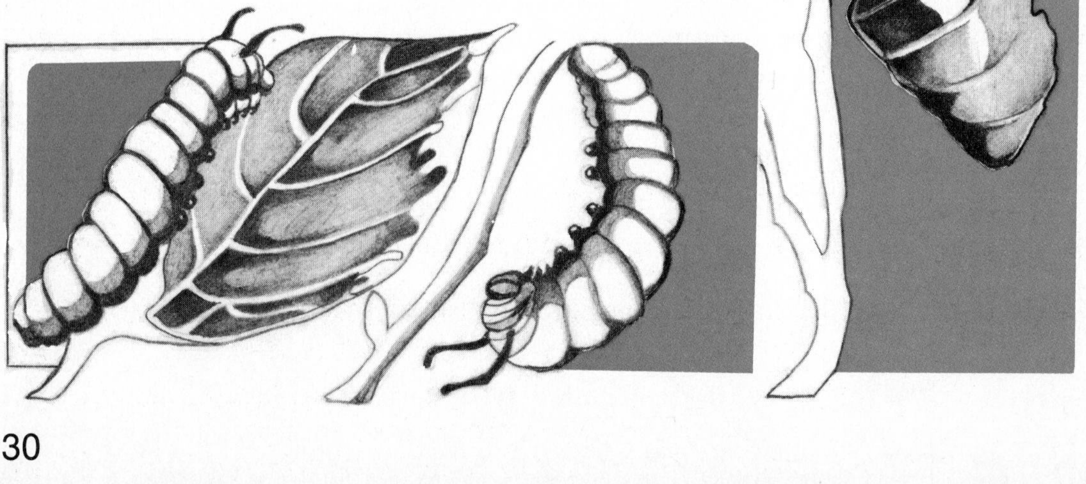

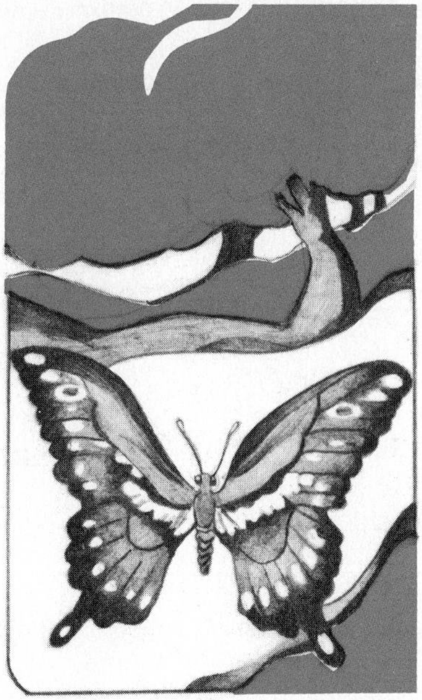

of silk button. The thread is attached to the bottom. Then the caterpillar ties itself fast to the stem. It throws the silk thread around both its body and the stem a few times. In time, its skin, which for many kinds of butterflies has bright colors and patterns, falls off. Underneath there is a shell. It turns brown.

When the weather turns warm, something wonderful happens. The shell bursts, and the butterfly pulls itself out. At first, it is very weak and cannot move its wings. After a few hours, it grows strong. The wide wings begin to move. Then, away it sails into the air!

B-4 Testing Yourself

NUMBER RIGHT

Draw a line under the right answer or fill in the blank.

1. A butterfly lays its eggs on the underside of a ______________________.

2. From the story, you can tell that
   a. butterflies form in their shells during the winter.
   b. caterpillars can fly in the spring.
   c. caterpillars eat harmful insects.

3. This story as a whole is about
   a. growing plants.
   b. raising silkworms for silk.
   c. caterpillars and butterflies.
   d. the weather and how it changes.

4. Butterflies turn into fat, green worms. Yes No Does not say

5. Butterflies have short lives. Yes No Does not say

6. What word in the first sentence means about the same as **turn into?**

____

Getting Ready to Read

SAY AND KNOW

Venus
flytrap
steel
stickers
needles
discover
suddenly
edge
fingers

Draw a line under the right answer or fill in the blank.

1. **Something that catches flies** is **a** **spring** **flytrap** **sticker.**
2. It is a very hard metal. **stickers** **needles** **steel**
3. They are parts of our hands. **fingers** **needles** **stickers**
4. **To find** means **to** **sticker** **fingers** **discover.**
5. It means **the side.** **spring** **steel** **edge**
6. If it happens without warning, it happens

______________.

B-5 A Strange Trap

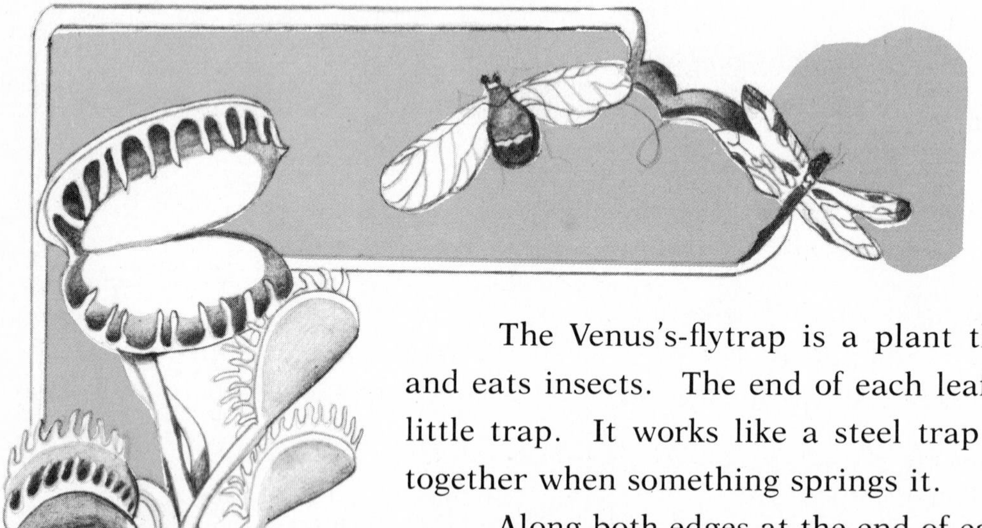

The Venus's-flytrap is a plant that catches and eats insects. The end of each leaf is really a little trap. It works like a steel trap that snaps together when something springs it.

Along both edges at the end of each leaf is a row of stickers. They are sharp, like needles. When this part of the leaf is open, you can see three little hairlike things on it.

Flies land on the leaf to eat a purple juice that they find there. When it enters the trap, the fly touches one of these hairlike things. The edges of this part of the leaf suddenly snap together. The rows of needles along the edges then cross each other, in the same way that you can cross the fingers of your two hands. These crossed needles keep the insect from getting out. Venus's-flytrap plants live on the flies and other insects caught in this way.

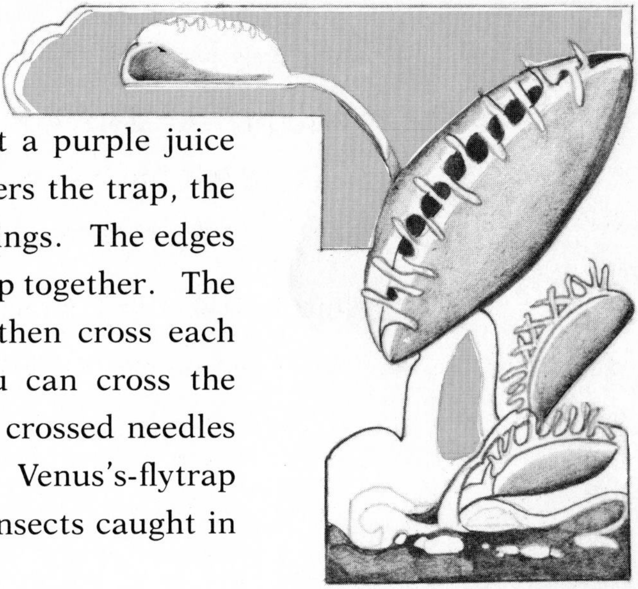

B-5 Testing Yourself

NUMBER RIGHT

Draw a line under the right answer or fill in the blank.

1. Some plants eat ______________________.
2. From the story, you can tell that
   a. flies take the juice of the flytrap.
   b. Venus's-flytraps only catch flies.
   c. only Venus's-flytraps catch flies.
3. This story as a whole is about
   a. flies and other insects.
   b. an insect-eating plant.
   c. traps.
   d. catching flies.
4. Venus's-flytraps grow in South Carolina. Yes No Does not say
5. Venus's-flytraps catch insects with their stems. Yes No Does not say
6. What word in the second paragraph, first sentence, means about the same as **line?** ____________

Getting Ready to Read

SAY AND KNOW

Massachusetts
poet
historian
colony
colonies
slave
obey
record
expect

Draw a line under the right answer or fill in the blank.

1. **Writings to keep for future use** are **a record colony poet.**
2. **Someone who studies history** is **a poet colony historian.**
3. **To follow the rules** is **to obey record colony.**
4. **A person who writes poetry** is **a slave poet law.**
5. The early states were called **colonies slaves historians.**
6. It is the name of a state. ____________________

B-6 Laws and Learning

In the 1700s, poor people worked hard to get along. Some of the laws made their lives harder. At that time, wives, servants, and children under 21 had to obey the head of the house. If they didn't, the law said they could be beaten.

In those days, poor people didn't expect to go to school. There were laws that said that black slaves should not be taught to read and write.

Even so, some slaves who wanted to learn were able to find people who would teach them.

With no public schools, many people had to find their own ways to learn. Hannah Adams and Mercy Otis Warren became historians without going to school. George Wythe learned Greek and Latin from his mother. Wythe became a law teacher. One of his students was Thomas Jefferson.

Lucy Terry was a slave in Massachusetts. She, too, found teachers for herself. She was one of the few black women to leave a record of what life was like in the American colonies. She may have been the first black poet in America.

B-6 Testing Yourself

NUMBER RIGHT

Draw a line under the right answer or fill in the blank.

1. When you do what someone tells you, you ______________.
2. From the story, you can tell that
   a. people don't give up if they really want to learn.
   b. people don't like to study in school.
   c. most people are poets and teachers.
3. This story as a whole is about
   a. how to be a teacher.
   b. laws and learning in the 1700s.
   c. how Massachusetts became a state.
   d. reading Latin and Greek.
4. A slave may have been the first black poet. Yes No Does not say
5. Laws never change. Yes No Does not say
6. What word in the second paragraph, first sentence, means the same as **look forward to?** ______________

Getting Ready to Read

SAY AND KNOW

arithmetic
subtract
multiply
divide
problems
correctly
directions
details
unimportant
suppose
connect
noticing

Draw a line under the right answer or fill in the blank.

1. **The study of numbers** is
   unimportant directions arithmetic.
2. To do something right is to do it
   noticing correctly multiply.
3. **Small parts of a whole** are details directions notices.
4. **Instructions in how to do anything** are
   details directions notices.
5. It means about the same as **imagine.**
   noticing subtract suppose
6. **The opposite of important** is ____________________.

B-7 Reading for Arithmetic

Some girls and boys know many arithmetic facts. These young people can add and subtract and multiply and divide. But they still have trouble with arithmetic. They cannot read the problems correctly. To do this well, you need to learn to read directions. You must also read all the details, even details that seem unimportant.

Suppose you were asked to do this:

Draw a line across a page. The line should be straight and 2 centimeters (about 4/5 inch) long. Now draw a line below each end of this line, going downward. The new lines should each be the same length as the top one. Your drawing should look

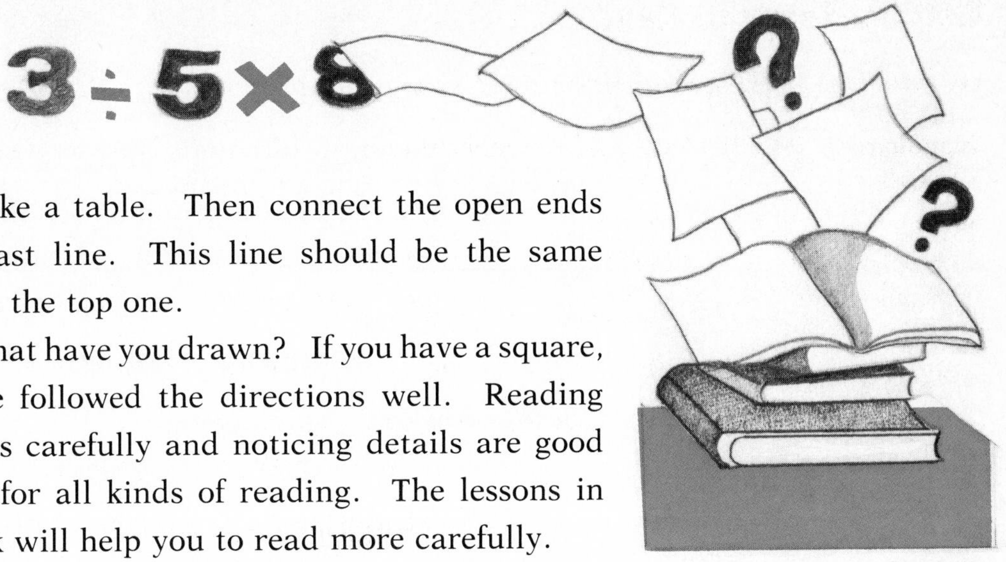

a little like a table. Then connect the open ends with a last line. This line should be the same length as the top one.

What have you drawn? If you have a square, you have followed the directions well. Reading directions carefully and noticing details are good practice for all kinds of reading. The lessons in this book will help you to read more carefully.

B-7 Testing Yourself

NUMBER RIGHT

Draw a line under the right answer or fill in the blank.

1. It is easier to read arithmetic problems if you can read

________________________.

2. From the story, you can tell that

a. arithmetic is an easy subject.
b. reading helps in all our work.
c. reading is unimportant.

3. This story as a whole is about

a. reading.
b. arithmetic.
c. reading arithmetic problems.
d. reading storybooks.

4. It is good to read carefully. Yes No Does not say

5. Most of the time, details are unimportant. Yes No Does not say

6. What word in the first paragraph, third sentence, means about the same as **difficulty?** ________________________

Getting Ready to Read

SAY AND KNOW

Scandinavian
custom
famous
Norwegian
crowded
culture
Minnesota
Swedish
Norway
Rolvaag
bitter
author

Draw a line under the right answer.

1. It means **very well known.** **famous** **bitter** **custom**
2. It means **a habit or practice that a group of people follow.** **custom** **famous** **bitter**
3. The language of Norway is **Minnesota** **culture** **Norwegian.**
4. **Containing a lot of people** means **being** **cultural** **crowded** **Swedish.**
5. It means **sharp** or **very unpleasant.** **custom** **culture** **bitter**
6. People from Sweden are **Swedish** **Norway** **Minnesota.**

B-8 A Wilderness Choice

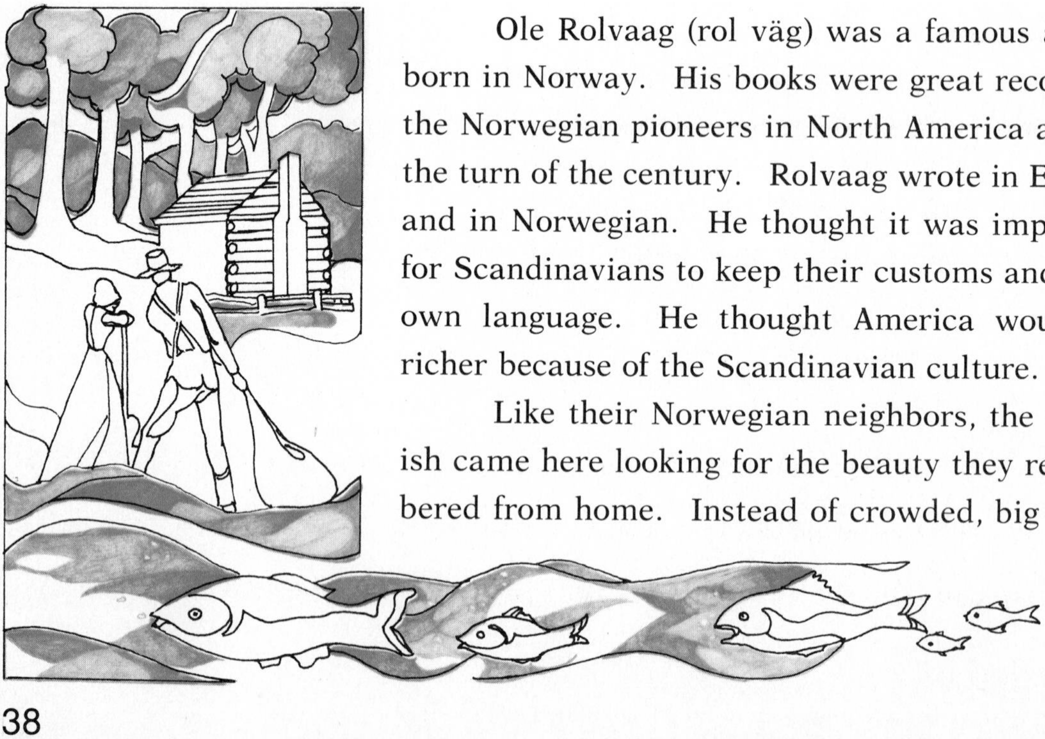

Ole Rolvaag (rol väg) was a famous author born in Norway. His books were great records of the Norwegian pioneers in North America around the turn of the century. Rolvaag wrote in English and in Norwegian. He thought it was important for Scandinavians to keep their customs and their own language. He thought America would be richer because of the Scandinavian culture.

Like their Norwegian neighbors, the Swedish came here looking for the beauty they remembered from home. Instead of crowded, big cities,

they wanted hillsides and lakes. They kept moving northwest to the wilderness of Minnesota.

With only a few pennies in their pockets, the Scandinavians began to work the land. Some families had to share their houses with other families. They all worked until they made enough money to build their own homes.

Families often had ten or more children. Many of them died from sickness. One woman told of the bitter cold in her cabin. In the winter, she wrote, her sheets froze and her pillow was covered with frost!

B-8 Testing Yourself

NUMBER RIGHT

Draw a line under the right answer or fill in the blank.

1. Scandinavians moved northwest to the wilderness of

____________________.

2. From the story, you can tell that
   a. Scandinavians hate the woods.
   b. traveling in Norway is fun.
   c. Scandinavian pioneers had a hard life.

3. This story as a whole is about
   a. Scandinavian pioneers.
   b. building houses.
   c. crowded cities.
   d. winters in Norway.

4. Scandinavian pioneers were rich. Yes No Does not say

5. Scandinavians had small families. Yes No Does not say

6. What word in the first sentence means **someone who writes stories?**

____

Getting Ready to Read

SAY AND KNOW	Draw a line under the right answer or fill in the blank.
safety	1. It means **before anything else.** **rule** **first** **afterward**
first	2. **A guide to how we act** is a **rule** **intersection** **safety.**
rule	3. **A crossing** is an **example** **afterward** **intersection.**
example	4. It means **the opposite of before.** **first** **afterward** **rule**
afterward	5. **To show a sample of a thing** is to give **a reminder** **a first** **an example.**
remainder	
intersection	6. It means the same as **freedom from harm.** ________

B-9 Safety First

Sometimes it's hard to think about safety first. If you do, you may keep from getting hurt and from hurting others. Here is one safety rule: Do not run into the street after a ball; first, make sure that no cars are coming. Here is another safety rule: Cross the street only at the intersection.

There are many other safety rules. For example, Sarah and Fred were building a doghouse. They were having a lot of fun. Soon it was time for dinner. Without a thought, off they ran. A little while afterward, Aunt Hannah came up the walk. She saw some boards with nails sticking up, and she carefully turned each of these boards face down. When Sarah and Fred came out after dinner, they were surprised to find their boards stuck

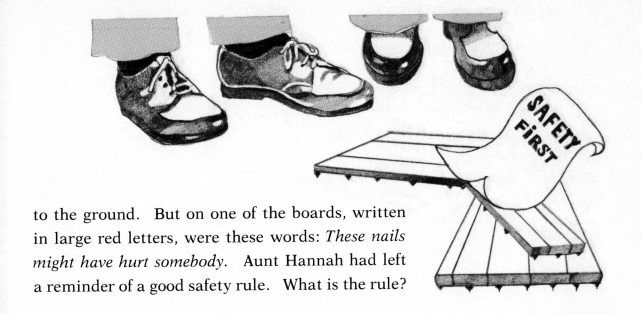

to the ground. But on one of the boards, written in large red letters, were these words: *These nails might have hurt somebody.* Aunt Hannah had left a reminder of a good safety rule. What is the rule?

B-9 Testing Yourself

NUMBER RIGHT

Draw a line under the right answer or fill in the blank.

1. There are many rules of ____________________.
2. From the story, you can tell that
   a. people can be careless.
   b. Aunt Hannah was angry.
   c. it is hard to build a doghouse.
3. This story as a whole is about
   a. thinking about safety.
   b. building things.
   c. making up rules.
   d. fixing dinner.
4. It is a good idea to know safety rules. Yes No Does not say
5. It is all right to cross streets in the middle of the block.
   Yes No Does not say
6. What word in the first paragraph, fourth sentence, means **crossing?**

____

Circus Family

Papa Ernesto and Mama Victoria had a special family. There were dozens of children and grandchildren, and they all worked in the same place. In fact, dozens of people in this family had been doing the same work for dozens of years.

The family was the Cristianis. Their work was with the circus. Actually, to this family, the circus was more than their work. It was a way of life.

The talent of the Cristianis was passed on from generation to generation. In Italy, the famous Cristianis fascinated audiences. Each one had a speciality. Lucio was famous for his backward flip onto a horse. Ortans was the first woman to do a triple somersault onto a high, high chair.

The talents and skills were passed on. The life of the circus stayed in the family. Cousins married one another. The Cristianis family grew. The little ones learned their acts young. Some joined the act under the big top when they were three.

Mama and Papa liked keeping the members of their family close to each other. They liked the big family act. Some of the children, though, wanted their own glory. It was fine to be part of the family act. But they wanted more.

Young Chita had thoughts like these. She dreamed about being queen of the circus.

When she was nine, Chita went off with her little horse, Mimi. Chita practiced jumping up and down on Mimi's back. She thought, "A queen's act is beginning." But the jumps were hardly an outstanding circus act. What else could she do? A ballerina! That was it! Chita would dance gracefully on her horse's back.

So the future queen began her hard work. Signora Bedini became her teacher. Every day, for hours, the practice went on. Chita had to pretend she was in a tiny closet. Over and over, she repeated her movements until they were graceful as well as correct. When she had her steps worked out, it was time for her to train her horse, as all bareback riders did.

So the partnership began. Chita and her horse worked together for 25 years. Their act became famous. And Chita did become one of the queens of the circus. Rich and poor came to cheer her act. Everyone seemed to love her.

The circus has been a spectacle of color and enchantment for thousands of years. Some people say that circus life is coming to an end. The circus is too expensive to run. And people are used to viewing extraordinary things just by turning on TV sets. The circus won't be a thrill anymore, they say. The reign of the queens and kings of the circus is over. What do you think?

MY READING TIME ______ (440 WORDS)

Thinking It Over

1. How did Chita show that she had a strong will?
2. Would the Cristianis have been as famous if they hadn't stuck together? Why or why not?
3. Were circus queens and kings great because of their dreams or because of hard work?

Getting Ready to Read

SAY AND KNOW

manufactured
factory
factories
machinery
prepared
cellars
spun
mills
inventors
invent
basement
storing

Draw a line under the right answer or fill in the blank.

1. If it has been made ready, it has been **invented** **prepared** **spun.**
2. **A large building where things are made** is **a** **factory** **machinery** **cellar.**
3. They are like **basements.** **factories** **mills** **cellars**
4. **To create** is about the same as **to** **mill** **invent** **prepare.**
5. Machines also may be called **mills** **machinery** **factories.**
6. It means about the same as **factories.** ________

C-1 Inventing New Ways

Once, men and women and girls and boys did much of their work with their hands. In those days, much of the food was prepared at home. Most homes had cellars for storing it. Today, foods like bread, butter, canned goods, meats, frozen foods, and many others are prepared in factories.

The spinning and weaving of cloth and the making of clothes were once done at home, too. Today, however, cloth is spun and woven in large mills. Clothing of all kinds is made in factories. Nearly everything we use or see in stores is made by people in factories with the help of machinery.

From the time of the early settlers, Americans have liked to invent things. At times, inventors have worked in their basements. Now many of them work for large companies that pay them to invent things. People in the United States have always found new ways and new machines to help them with their work.

C-1 Testing Yourself

NUMBER RIGHT

Draw a line under the right answer or fill in the blank.

1. Americans have always liked to ______________________.

2. From the story, you can tell that today
   a. most people have nothing to do.
   b. people have less to do at home then they once did.
   c. people do not like machines.

3. This story as a whole is about
   a. making clothes.
   b. storing food in cellars.
   c. preparing goods in the early days.
   d. making things, past and present.

4. Factories and machines make people lazy. Yes No Does not say

5. Machines do most of the work in a factory. Yes No Does not say

6. What word in the first paragraph, third sentence, means **keeping?**

____

Getting Ready to Read

SAY AND KNOW	Draw a line under the right answers or fill in the blank.
judged	**1.** Which two are fish? **potlatch** **salmon** **halibut**
wealth	
honor	**2. Someone who gives a party** is **the** **judge** **totem** **host.**
potlatch	**3.** It means **riches.** **potlatch** **honor** **wealth**
host	
salmon	**4. To show great respect** is **to** **judge** **contest** **honor.**
halibut	**5. Carved and painted posts** are called **leaders** **totems** **feasts.**
totem	
huge	**6.** Something that is **very big** is ________.

C-2 People of the Totem Poles

Among the native tribes of the Northwest Coast, rich people were greatly honored. Wealth was judged by how many things leaders could give away. To do this, they held feasts called *potlatches.* People from near and far were invited.

The high point of the potlatch came when the host gave away fine things to the guests. When you could do this, you showed that you were so powerful that you did not need anything.

The Northwest tribes were famous for their fishing. They caught whales, salmon, and halibut. They carved huge boats from giant trees. These boats, and the wooden houses of the Northwest, were painted with different colors and designs. Often the houses were large enough to hold 100 people. In front of their houses, families set tall posts with faces carved and painted on them. These posts, called *totems,* told the story of the families who lived in the houses.

C-2 Testing Yourself

NUMBER RIGHT

Draw a line under the right answer or fill in the blank.

1. At a potlatch, the host gave away ____________________.

2. From the story, you can tell that
   a. tribes of the Northwest Coast did not like to own things.
   b. some tribes liked to be poor.
   c. wealth played an important part in the lives of some tribes.

3. This story as a whole is about
   a. tribes of the Northwest.
   b. giving feasts.
   c. a Southwest custom.
   d. how to become rich.

4. Potlatches were a lot of fun. Yes No Does not say

5. Northwest tribes honored poor people. Yes No Does not say

6. What word in the first sentence means **treated with great respect?**

____

Getting Ready to Read

SAY AND KNOW

pioneers
notch
wooden
fiddle
enemy
neighbors
house-raising
plugged
peg

Draw a line under the right answer or fill in the blank.

1. **The opposite of friend** is **pioneer peg enemy.**
2. **People who live near you** are **pioneers neighbors unfriendly.**
3. **Another name for violin** is **neighbor fiddle wooden.**
4. It means **made out of wood. cabin wooden close**
5. **Getting together to build a house** is **a game story house-raising.**
6. It is **a piece of wood used like a nail.** ___________

C-3 Lending a Hand

In New England, pioneers often built their cabins close together for protection against wild animals and human enemies. But, farther to the west, pioneers' cabins often were built far apart.

When it was time to build a house, neighbors came from far and near to help. They cut down trees. Then the logs were notched to fit together tightly. Everybody worked. The strongest people lifted the logs into place. Some carved wooden pegs to serve as nails. Others plugged the spaces between the logs with clay, mud, and moss.

When the roof was finally on, it was time for a feast. There were games, contests, and storytelling. Usually, someone would bring a fiddle. Then there would be dancing and singing until late at night. A house-raising was a time for hard work and hard play, too!

C-3 Testing Yourself

NUMBER RIGHT

Draw a line under the right answer or fill in the blank.

1. Many pioneers made their houses of ________________.

2. From the story, you can tell that
   a. a house-raising took many weeks.
   b. pioneers were happy to get new neighbors.
   c. building a house was all work and no play.

3. This story as a whole is about
   a. pioneers in the new lands.
   b. carving fiddles.
   c. houses built far apart.
   d. building houses in new lands.

4. Pioneers used wooden pegs. Yes No Does not say

5. Log cabins were cool in summer. Yes No Does not say

6. What word in the second paragraph, third sentence, means **cut with a groove?** ________________

Getting Ready to Read

SAY AND KNOW	Draw a line under the right answer or fill in the blank.
jumper	**1.** This animal lives on land and in water. **frog** **tadpole** **hind**
frog	
hind	**2.** It means **come out.** **sniff** **full-grown** **appear**
web	**3.** It means **back** or **rear.** **hind** **jumper** **frog**
sniff	
lungs	**4.** Animals breathe with their **edges** **lungs** **frogs.**
appear	**5.** **The border of something** is its **edge** **lungs** **web.**
tadpole	**6.** When it is **as big as it will ever be,** it is
edge	
full-grown	______________________.

C-4 A Big Change

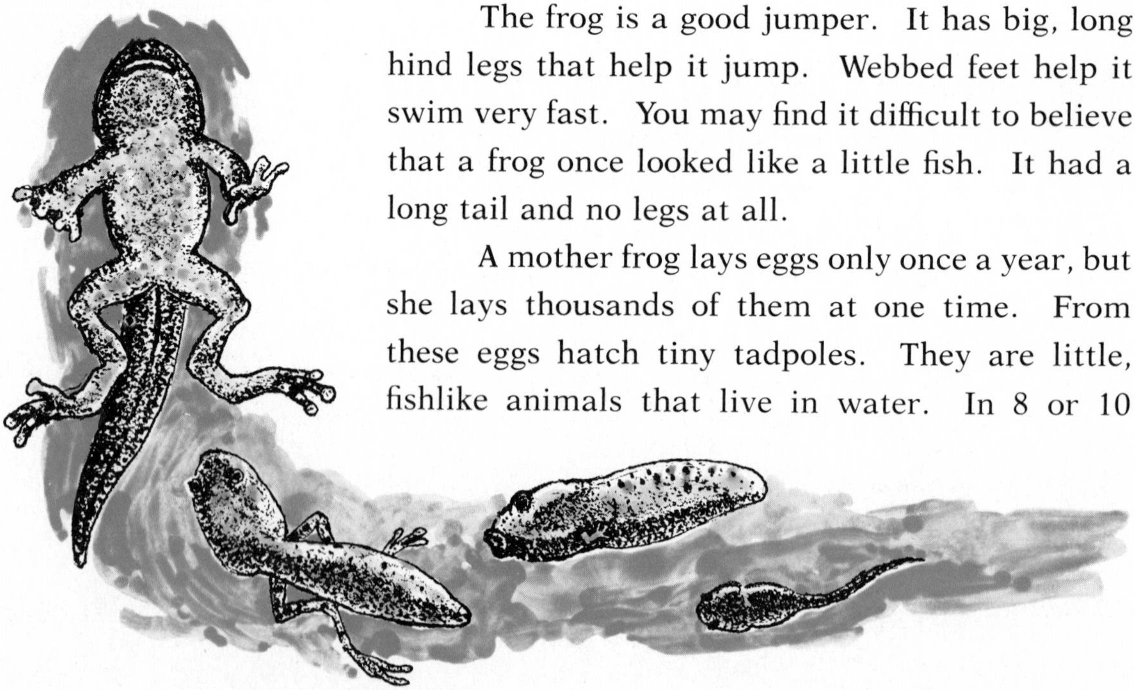

The frog is a good jumper. It has big, long hind legs that help it jump. Webbed feet help it swim very fast. You may find it difficult to believe that a frog once looked like a little fish. It had a long tail and no legs at all.

A mother frog lays eggs only once a year, but she lays thousands of them at one time. From these eggs hatch tiny tadpoles. They are little, fishlike animals that live in water. In 8 or 10

weeks, the tadpoles are full grown. They come to the edge of the water and sniff air into their small lungs. After a time, their lungs grow larger and their tails get smaller. Soon their legs appear.

In a few days, their tails are gone, and two strong hind legs with webbed feet have grown, as well as two front legs, or arms. The tadpoles have become frogs.

C-4 Testing Yourself

NUMBER RIGHT ______

Draw a line under the right answer or fill in the blank.

1. Frog eggs hatch into ______________________.

2. From the story, you can tell that
  a. the mother of a tadpole is a fish.
  b. the mother of a tadpole is a frog.
  c. the mother of a tadpole is neither a fish nor a frog.

3. This story as a whole is about
  a. the webbed feet of the frog.
  b. tadpoles changing into frogs.
  c. the tadpole's lungs getting larger.
  d. the frog laying eggs.

4. The frog has a tail. Yes No Does not say

5. The frog is a fast swimmer. Yes No Does not say

6. What word in the second paragraph, fifth sentence, means about the same as **breathe?** ____________

Getting Ready to Read

SAY AND KNOW

except
true
fog
moist
southern
moss
leaves
roots
thrive
surprised

Draw a line under the right answer or fill in the blank.

1. It means **the opposite of false.** **moss** **fog** **true**
2. It means about the same as **wet.** **true** **fog** **moist**
3. They are **parts of a plant.** **moss** **fog** **leaves**
4. **Parts of a plant growing under the ground** are **food** **thrive** **roots.**
5. It means **do very well.** **surprise** **moist** **thrive**
6. A great deal of water in the air can make **a heavy mist** or **a** ____________________.

C-5 Living on Air

Most plants have roots that grow in the ground or in the water. But there are some plants that thrive without any roots. Such plants live and grow in the air. Some people think that such plants have no food except the air. That is not true. The plants also get food that is carried on dust and fog. They get water from the rain, too.

In the warm, moist, southern part of our country, many trees have a great deal of Spanish "moss." This is not really moss. Instead, it is many air plants growing close together.

The young air plants grow from leaves. Put one of the leaves of an air plant on the ground, or hang it up in a room. Soon, a lot of baby plants will grow from the edges of the leaf.

C-5 Testing Yourself

NUMBER RIGHT

Draw a line under the right answer or fill in the blank.

1. The young air plants grow from ______________________.
2. From the story, you can tell that
   a. air plants differ from other plants in many ways.
   b. air plants grow more slowly than other plants.
   c. air plants eat insects.
3. This story as a whole is about
   a. air plants.
   b. Spanish "moss."
   c. air plants getting food.
   d. growing baby air plants.
4. Hanging "moss" is an air plant and a moss. Yes No Does not say
5. Some air plants hang from trees. Yes No Does not say
6. What word in the second paragraph, first sentence, means about the same as **nation?** ______________________

Getting Ready to Read

SAY AND KNOW	Draw a line under the right answer or fill in the blank.
musician	**1.** Someone who is **well known** is **famous** **symphony** **jazz.**
famous	**2. A person who knows a great deal about music** is **a musician** **an orchestra** **an idea.**
mixing	
orchestra	**3.** If you lead or direct something, you are a **ballet** **director** **jazz.**
idea	
jazz	**4.** It means **a group of people playing music.** **ballet** **director** **orchestra**
symphony	**5. Putting together** is about the same as **mixing** **ballet** **famous.**
director	
ballet	**6.** It means about the same as **thought.** ________

C-6 The Queen of Jazz

Many call her the Queen of Jazz. Her name is Mary Lou Williams. In the 1930s, she wrote songs and played the piano. Her jazz music made her famous. She played in the top jazz clubs. She

worked with other great musicians. Through the years, she wrote about 400 songs.

For a while, she forgot about being famous. She spent a great deal of time in church. Then she began to work on a new music idea. She mixed the music of the church with her jazz music.

Great symphony orchestras and ballet companies played her new music. The dance director Alvin Ailey liked to use black music as the center of his dances. His famous dance company used Williams' Jazz Mass for a ballet called "Mary Lou's Mass."

Mary Lou Williams is happy about mixing jazz and church music. To her, real jazz has love.

C-6 Testing Yourself

NUMBER RIGHT ______

Draw a line under the right answer or fill in the blank.

1. Mary Lou Williams was called the Queen of __________.

2. From the story, you can tell that
   a. Mary Lou Williams gave up music forever.
   b. Mary Lou Williams liked to dance best.
   c. Mary Lou Williams spent many years writing music.

3. This story as a whole is about
   a. church music.   c. jazz clubs.
   b. being famous.   d. a great musician.

4. Mary Lou liked to sing.   Yes   No   Does not say

5. Mary Lou Williams found a way to mix jazz and church music.
Yes   No   Does not say

6. What word in the last sentence means **not fake?** __________

Getting Ready to Read

SAY AND KNOW

circle

square

corner

angles

triangle

rectangle

rectangular

hexagon

Draw a line under the right answer or fill in the blanks.

1. Which word is made from the word **rectangle?**

triangle **circle** **rectangular**

2. **A corner where lines meet** is called

a square **an angle** **a circle.**

3. **A shape with no angles** is a **corner** **square** **circle.**

4. The word part **rect-** means "right." Write the words with this syllable. ____________ ____________

5. Write the two words that end with **angle.**

____________ ____________

C-7 What Do You Call That Shape?

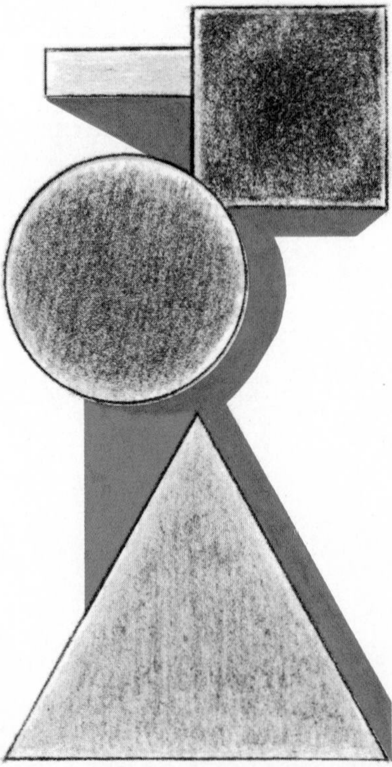

How many kinds of shapes can you name? If something is flat and round, what do you call it? You call it a circle. What can you see around you that looks like a circle?

Another flat shape is a square. A square has four sides. Each side is the same length. A square has four corners called *right angles*.

A triangle is also flat. The prefix *tri-* on the base word *angle* means "three." A triangle always has three sides and three angles.

All the pages of this book have four square corners, but the pages are not square. Can you tell why not? It is because the sides of each page are longer than the ends. Shapes like this are rectangles. You can say that they are rectangular shapes.

Do you know the names of other flat shapes? Try to find out what a hexagon looks like. Soon you will learn the names of shapes that are not flat. Do you know any of these names now?

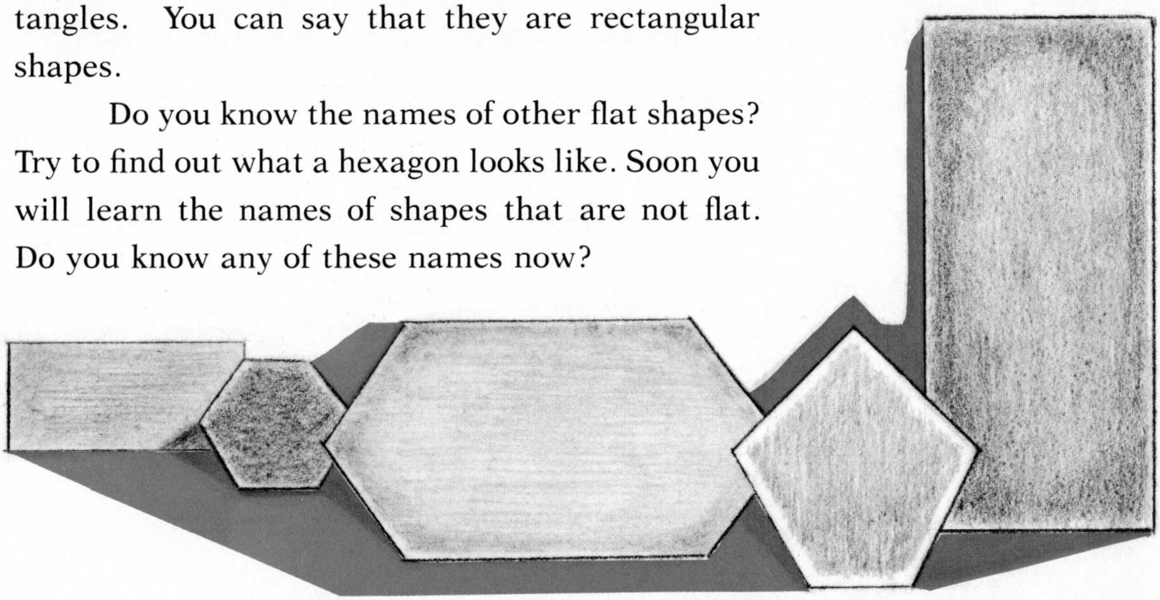

C-7 Testing Yourself

NUMBER RIGHT

Draw a line under the right answer or fill in the blank.

1. Something round and flat is called a ______________________.

2. From the story, you can tell that
   a. only shapes with four sides of equal length can be squares.
   b. shapes with five sides are called triangles.
   c. all shapes with curved sides are circles.

3. This story as a whole is about
   a. shapes called triangles.
   b. the names of different shapes.
   c. books and pages.
   d. lines and circles.

4. Some shapes are flat. Yes No Does not say

5. Squares are flat shapes. Yes No Does not say

6. What word in the last paragraph, third sentence, means **find out?**

____

Getting Ready to Read

SAY AND KNOW

Cuba
Cubans
cigar
skill
treat
custard
background
colorful

Draw a line under the right answer or fill in the blank.

1. **A kind of dessert** is **a** **custard** **treat** **cigar.**
2. **People's past** is their **background** **skill** **custard.**
3. Knowing how to do something well is **a** **treat** **skill** **cigar.**
4. **People who come from Cuba** are called **colorful** **skilled** **Cubans.**
5. Candy is often called **a** **skill** **custard** **treat.**
6. It means **full of color** ______________.

C-8 Neighborhoods Like Home

Over the past 20 years, many Cubans have come to the United States to live. Some have settled in Texas and California. Others settled in New York and Florida. Since Miami is close to Cuba, many have made their homes there.

Often, Cubans have grouped together to be with others who share the same background. In many ways, the Cuban neighborhoods in Miami

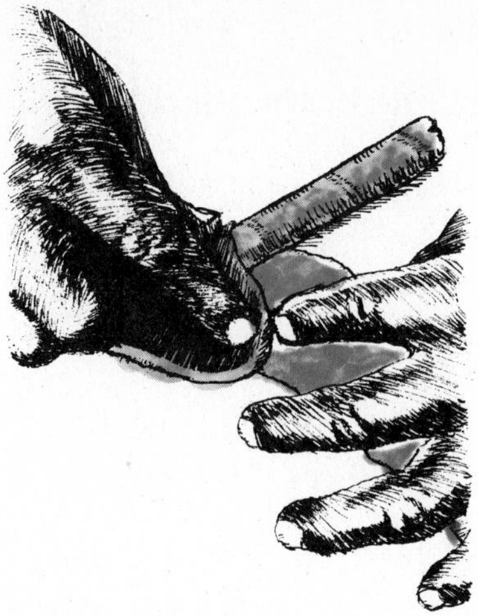

look like neighborhoods in Cuba. Instead of having large stores, the streets are lined with small, colorful shops. Many signs are written in Spanish. You might see the word *bodega* (bō dā′ ga) instead of "grocery store."

The Cubans want to keep their own way of life. But they are an important part of American life, too. Some are shop owners and bankers. Others bring old skills with them, like knowing how to roll cigars by hand.

These immigrants bring new food ideas to the United States, too. Now a lot of grocery stores carry black beans, yellow rice, and mixes for a special custard called *flan.* These Spanish-American treats are for everyone to enjoy!

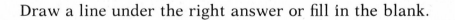

C-8 Testing Yourself

NUMBER RIGHT

Draw a line under the right answer or fill in the blank.

1. Miami is very close to ______________________.

2. From the story, you can tell that
   a. Cubans have added new things to American life.
   b. Cubans don't want to remember their backgrounds.
   c. Miami is too hot for most Cubans.

3. This story as a whole is about
   a. Cubans who have settled in America.
   b. learning how to roll cigars.
   c. making yellow rice.
   d. opening a grocery store.

4. It is easy to make Cuban treats. Yes No Does not say

5. Most Cuban stores are very large. Yes No Does not say

6. What word in the last sentence means **be happy with?** ___________

Getting Ready to Read

SAY AND KNOW	Draw a line under the right answer or fill in the blank.
fuel	1. **Something that is good for your health** is
healthy	**healthy** **plain** **bothered.**
popular	2. If many people like it, it is **popular** **yogurt** **fuel.**
protein	3. **To mix** is **to** **heat** **stir** **bother.**
Balkan	4. It is **the opposite of cooled.** **fuel** **popular** **heated**
yogurt	5. **Something that keeps an engine going** is
bothered	**Balkan** **protein** **fuel.**
heated	
stir	6. It means **disturbed.** ____________________

C-9 Eating the Right Foods

Most boys and girls don't think about the kinds of foods they eat. But to be healthy, you need the right kinds of food. You know that an engine runs on fuel. Our bodies also need fuel on which to run. Fuel for the body comes from foods high in protein. These are foods like meat, eggs, nuts, and milk.

Yogurt is a healthy food made from milk. In the Balkan countries, people have been eating yogurt for years and years. They say that they live long, healthy lives because of the yogurt.

Yogurt is now popular in this country. Some people even like to make their own. To do this, you need milk and a little bit of plain yogurt. Heat the milk until it almost boils. Then cool it in a

bowl for about 25 minutes. Next you stir in the yogurt and cover the bowl with a plate. The trick then is to keep the bowl in a warm place where it won't be bothered. In 8 to 12 hours, you will have a bowl of yogurt, instead of milk!

C-9 Testing Yourself

NUMBER RIGHT

Draw a line under the right answer or fill in the blank.

1. Meat, eggs, nuts, and milk are called ______________________.
2. From the story, you can tell that
   a. we eat foods from far-off countries.
   b. too much milk is bad for you.
   c. meat is the best food for children.
3. This story as a whole is about
   a. eating between meals.
   b. growing up.
   c. healthy foods to eat.
   d. the wrong foods for children.
4. At dinner, we need two cups of milk. Yes No Does not say
5. Children should have yogurt every day. Yes No Does not say
6. What word in the first paragraph means **something that can be burned for energy?** ___________

A Clever Hunter

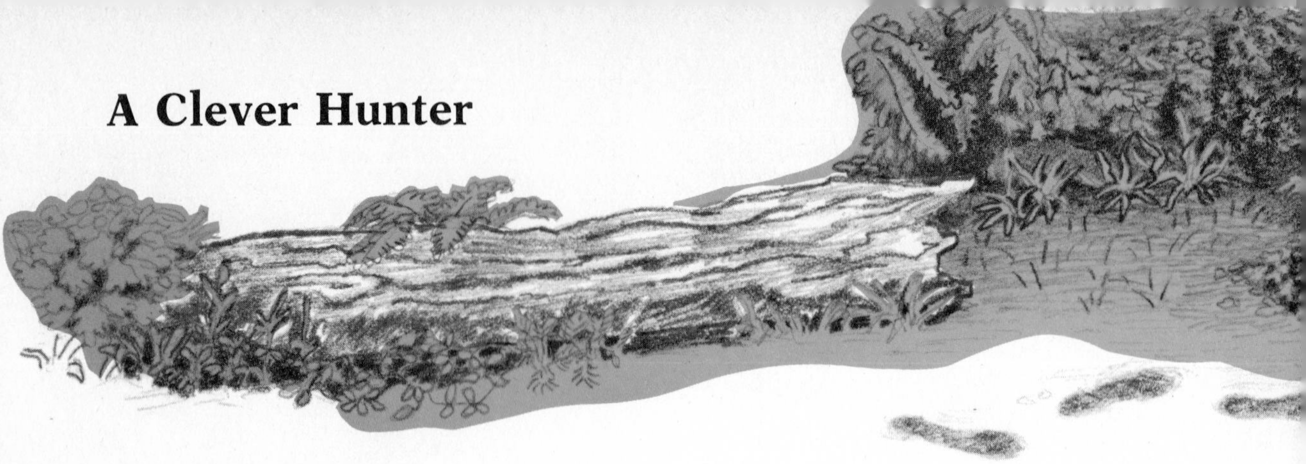

For many long hours, a Native American hunter followed the track of a deer. Finally, he came upon his game. He took careful aim. His arrow flew through the air, and the deer fell. Throwing the deer over his shoulders, the hunter started on the long journey home. It was nearly morning when he got to his wigwam. He hung the deer on a nearby tree and lay down to sleep.

The tired hunter slept deeply and for a long time. When he finally awoke, he ran to the tree where he had hung the deer. His animal was gone! The hunter had very sharp eyes. One look around was enough to tell him the whole story of the stolen deer.

Quickly he followed the trail to a camp that was nearby. Several men sat about the fire. The hunter told them that a white man had taken his deer. "The man is not here!" he cried, after looking at each of the men. "He is an old man. He had a gun and a little dog with a short tail."

"Well," said one man, "why didn't you go after him and get your deer?"

To the surprise of all, the hunter said that he had been sleeping when the deer was taken.

"Then how do you know that the man who took your deer was a white man?" they asked.

"A Native hunter walks so," answered the hunter. He pointed his toes straight ahead. "A white man walks so." He pointed his toes out. "They were a white man's tracks."

"How do you know this person was old?" they asked.

"A young man takes long steps. His tracks are far apart. An

old man takes short steps. His tracks are close together," the Native American replied. "These tracks are close."

"How do you know the old white man had a gun?"

"I saw the mark on the tree where the man leaned his gun while he got the deer," said the hunter.

"But how do you know that this old man with a gun had a little dog with a short tail?" the campers asked.

"I saw the place where the little dog sat to watch the man take the deer down," he replied. "The little dog wagged its tail. It made a mark on the ground. The mark was close to where the dog sat. So I know the little dog has a short tail."

Just then, a man came out of the woods. He was an old white man. He carried a gun. Close at his heels came a little dog with a short tail.

"That is the man," the hunter said.

"Yes," said one camper, "he is your thief. He took the deer, and he shall return it. A hunter who can track a deer both dead and alive should have his game."

Then, turning to the old man, the camper said, "Next time you are hungry for deer meat, follow the trail of a live deer as this hunter did."

MY READING TIME ______ (410 WORDS)

Thinking It Over

1. How was the old man unfair to the hunter?
2. How were the campers fair to the hunter?
3. Was the hunter fair to the others?

Getting Ready to Read

SAY AND KNOW

steam
oxygen
hydrogen
tank
gasoline
enough
regular
handle
power
plastic
mini-

Draw a line under the right answers or fill in the blank.

1. **Water in the form of a gas** is **steam** **gasoline** **power.**
2. Something strong has **steam** **power** **enough.**
3. **As much as is needed** is **handle** **airplane** **enough.**
4. Which two are gases? **hydrogen** **oxygen** **battery**
5. If it is **like all the others,** it is **regular** **mini-** **plastic.**
6. It means about the same as **manage** or **control.** ____________

D-1 Big Changes in Travel

Once, people used carts, buggies, and wagons for travel. As time passed, people found ways to use fuel to run engines. Coal and oil were burned to make steam that moved boats and trains.

Today, our big ocean liners and jet planes are moved by engines that burn fuel. Rockets that carry astronauts into space burn gases like oxygen and hydrogen.

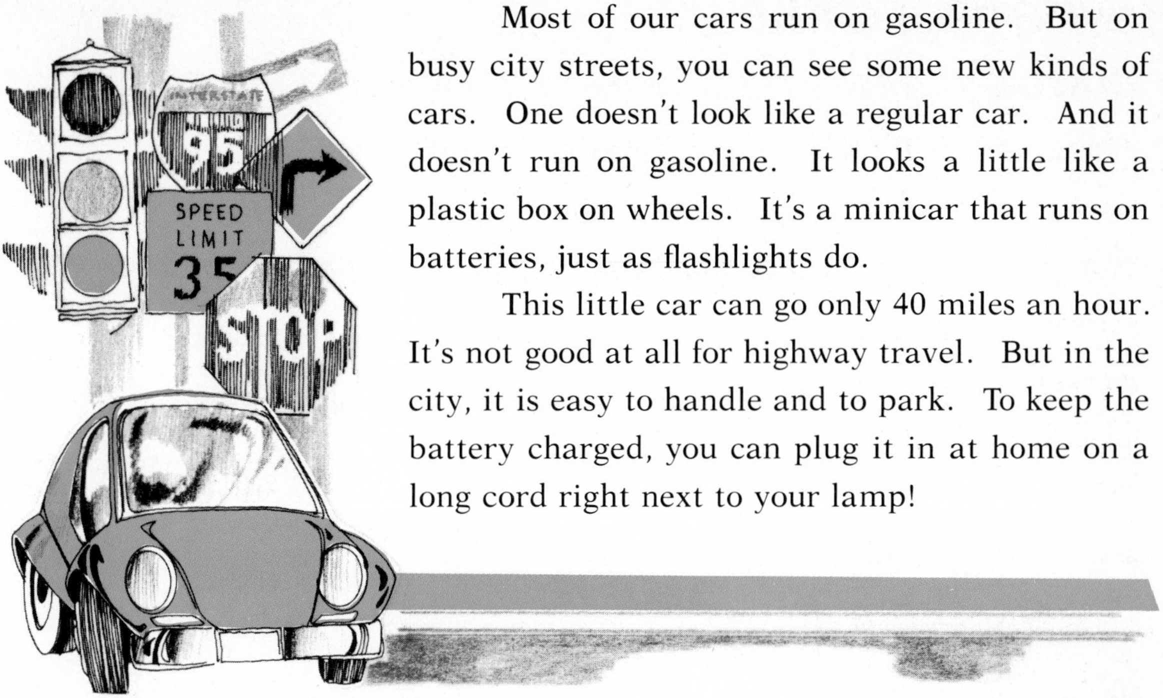

Most of our cars run on gasoline. But on busy city streets, you can see some new kinds of cars. One doesn't look like a regular car. And it doesn't run on gasoline. It looks a little like a plastic box on wheels. It's a minicar that runs on batteries, just as flashlights do.

This little car can go only 40 miles an hour. It's not good at all for highway travel. But in the city, it is easy to handle and to park. To keep the battery charged, you can plug it in at home on a long cord right next to your lamp!

D-1 Testing Yourself

NUMBER RIGHT

Draw a line under the right answer or fill in the blank.

1. Most cars today run on ________________.

2. From the story, you can tell that
   a. we keep finding more ways to run engines.
   b. automobiles, today, run on steam.
   c. coal is the best fuel for cars.

3. This story as a whole is about
   a. different fuels for engines.
   b. the buggies our grandparents used.
   c. the automobiles of yesterday.
   d. trains of yesterday and today.

4. Rockets traveling into space burn gases. Yes No Does not say

5. Gasoline is the cheapest fuel for engines. Yes No Does not say

6. What word in the last sentence means **full of energy?** ________________

Getting Ready to Read

SAY AND KNOW	
clothing	Draw a line under the right answer or fill in the blank.
layer	1. It means **bugs.** **insects** **skins** **clothing**
disease	2. **One thing on top of another** is **a** **skin** **layer** **hide.**
nomads	3. It means **animal skins.** **nomads** **layers** **hides**
shellfish	4. **People who move about** are **nomads** **insects** **layers.**
insects	5. It means **sickness.** **shellfish** **nomads** **disease**
hides	6. Which word is made up of two words and names a water
skins	animal? ____________________

D-2 Homes on the Plains

Tribes like the Plains Native People were nomads. They built homes that could be moved easily. Other tribes moved when they were bothered by problems like diseases or even insects.

Some tribes always changed homes when the seasons changed. In the spring, they lived near the fields, which the women planted. In the summer, they might move to the ocean, where the men fished and the women caught shellfish. In the winter, they moved to a deep valley to protect themselves.

Inside their homes, many people lived close together. Their homes were warm and cozy. There were no windows to let in cold air. Mats, rugs, and hides on the walls kept the cold out.

The Native Americans knew other ways to protect themselves from cold and insects. They often put a layer of bear fat or fish oil on their skin. That kept bugs away. It kept them warm, too. Very often, they needed little clothing to keep them warm, as long as they wore their special oils.

D-2 Testing Yourself

NUMBER RIGHT

Draw a line under the right answer or fill in the blank.

1. Native People who lived on the plains were ____________________.

2. From the story, you can tell that
   a. the tribes were ready for all weather.
   b. the tribes never knew how to keep warm.
   c. fishing was the favorite sport.

3. This story as a whole is about
   a. building houses.
   b. nomad tribes.
   c. making fish oils.
   d. keeping insects away.

4. Native Americans who lived on the plains liked to move.
Yes No Does not say

5. Many Native Americans wore bear fat. Yes No Does not say

6. What word in the second sentence means **without difficulty?** __________

Getting Ready to Read

SAY AND KNOW

striking
flint
spark
oven
homemade
greased
ashes
managed
kettle

Draw a line under the right answer or fill in the blank.

1. **Handled** or **controlled** means **matched** **managed** **homemade.**
2. It is **a very hard stone.** **an oven** **heat** **a flint**
3. **A small bit of fire** is a **match** **spark** **flint.**
4. **A stove for baking** is **an oven** **ashes** **a flint.**
5. **What is left after something has been burned** is called **heating** **matches** **ashes.**
6. **Something made at home** is ______________________.

D-3 Frontier Homes

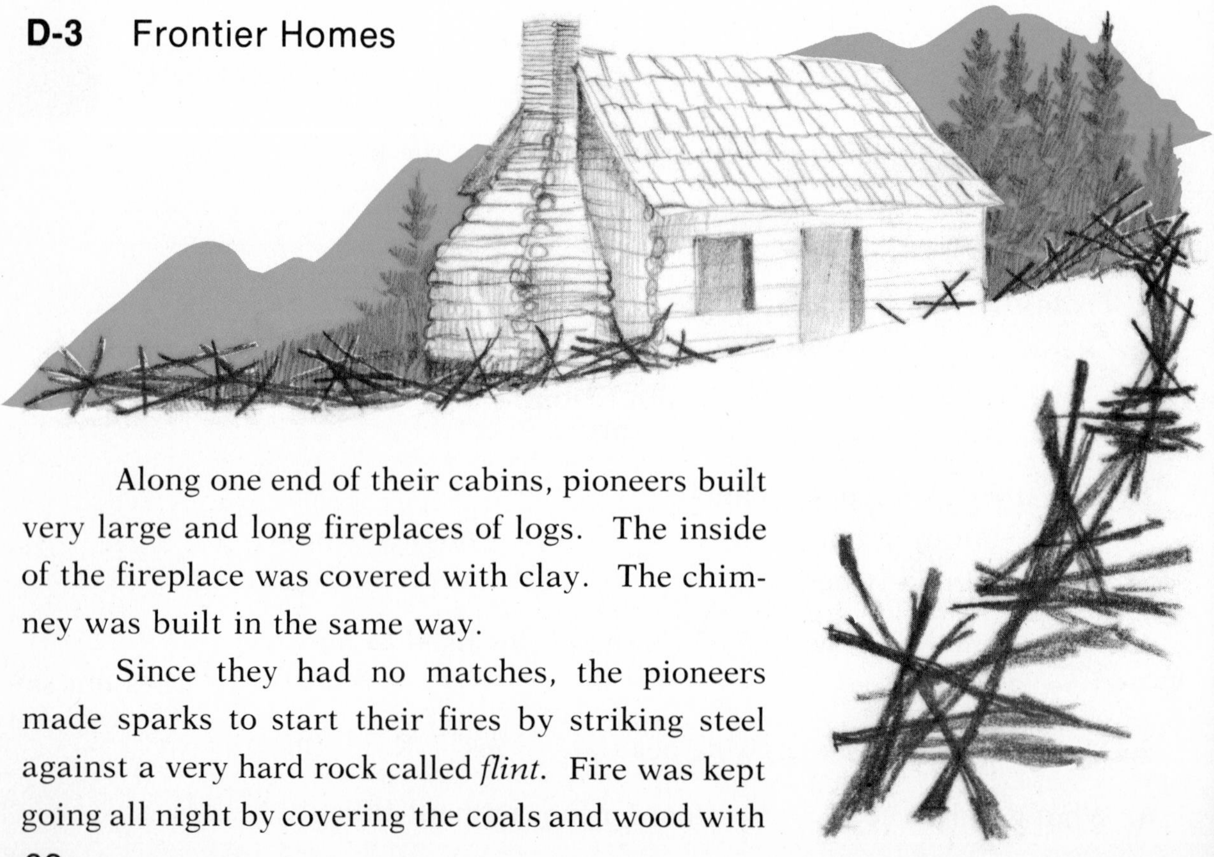

Along one end of their cabins, pioneers built very large and long fireplaces of logs. The inside of the fireplace was covered with clay. The chimney was built in the same way.

Since they had no matches, the pioneers made sparks to start their fires by striking steel against a very hard rock called *flint.* Fire was kept going all night by covering the coals and wood with ashes. If the fire did go out, a child might be sent to a neighbor to get some hot coals with which to start another fire.

Because pioneers had no stoves, they used their fireplaces for cooking as well as for heating the houses. They hung pots and kettles over the hot coals in the fireplace. They even managed to bake bread without an oven. In time, they often built a stone or brick oven into the chimney.

Furniture was mostly homemade. In place of nails, the pioneers used wooden pegs. In place of window glass, they used greased paper or animal skins.

D-3 Testing Yourself

NUMBER RIGHT

Draw a line under the right answer or fill in the blank.

1. Besides heating, the fireplace was used for ________________.

2. From the story, you can tell that
   a. pioneers did not like to cook.
   b. it was difficult to make fires.
   c. pioneers could not bake bread.

3. This story as a whole is about
   a. building a fireplace.
   b. the pioneers and their food.
   c. the pioneers' fireplaces.
   d. starting a fire without matches.

4. The pioneers cooked outside in the summer. Yes No Does not say

5. A pioneer could start a fire without matches. Yes No Does not say

6. What word in the last sentence means **covered with oil?**

____

Getting Ready to Read

SAY AND KNOW	Draw a line under the right answer or fill in the blank.
woodpecker	**1.** It is **a kind of bird.** **harmful** **woodpecker** **Pacific**
Pacific	**2.** It is **the name of an ocean.** **Pacific** **probe** **control**
harmful	**3. One who makes something grow** is called **a**
grower	**tongue** **grower** **probe.**
probe	**4. Dig into** means **harm** **noise** **probe.**
control	**5.** It means about the same as **to keep something down.**
noises	**juicy** **sharp** **control**
sharp	**6.** It is **the opposite of dull.** ____________

D-4 Black, Red, and White

There are many different kinds of woodpeckers in North America. The people in the east, south, and middle parts of our country know best the kind with the red head, black back, and white breast. But this bird is not found in the states of the Pacific Coast.

Without knowing it, woodpeckers help us control insects. The birds feed on worms and insects, many of which are harmful to trees. Woodpeckers have sharp, strong bills with which they probe the wood for insects. They have long tongues with sharp ends. First the woodpecker digs into the wood with its sharp bill. Then it reaches in with its tongue and pulls out the worm or insect. Sometimes, woodpeckers also eat the juicy fruit that grows on the trees. Then, the fruit grower doesn't like woodpeckers.

Woodpeckers, unlike other birds, do not have lovely songs. Woodpeckers make noises that are not pleasant.

D-4 Testing Yourself

NUMBER RIGHT

Draw a line under the right answer or fill in the blank.

1. The woodpecker pulls out the worm or insect with its ____________.

2. From the story, you can tell that

a. woodpeckers are our enemies.

b. woodpeckers are always singing.

c. woodpeckers can be helpful to growers.

3. This story as a whole is about

a. the woodpecker.

b. the color of woodpeckers.

c. the tongues of woodpeckers.

d. woodpeckers doing harm to trees.

4. The red-headed woodpecker is found along the Pacific Coast.

Yes No Does not say

5. Woodpeckers do more good than harm. Yes No Does not say

6. What word in the first sentence means **types?** ____________

Getting Ready to Read

SAY AND KNOW

dandelion
blossom
float
cattail
weak
scattering
flyaway
approaches
loose
breeze

Draw a line under the right answer or fill in the blank.

1. It is **the opposite of strong.** **blossom** **dandelion** **weak**
2. **A small wind** is called **a** **breeze** **cattail** **float.**
3. **To be carried by the wind** is **to** **blossom** **approach** **float.**
4. If something gets closer, it **looses** **scatters** **approaches.**
5. It is **the opposite of tight.** **breeze** **loose** **weak**
6. **Throwing here and there** means ____________________.

D-5 Floating Umbrellas

Each plant has its own way of scattering its seeds. When the dandelion blossom becomes white and light, the seeds are getting ready to fly away. Every dandelion seed has a tiny umbrella at one end. This shape helps it to float off on the wind. Watch the dandelion blossom as it turns

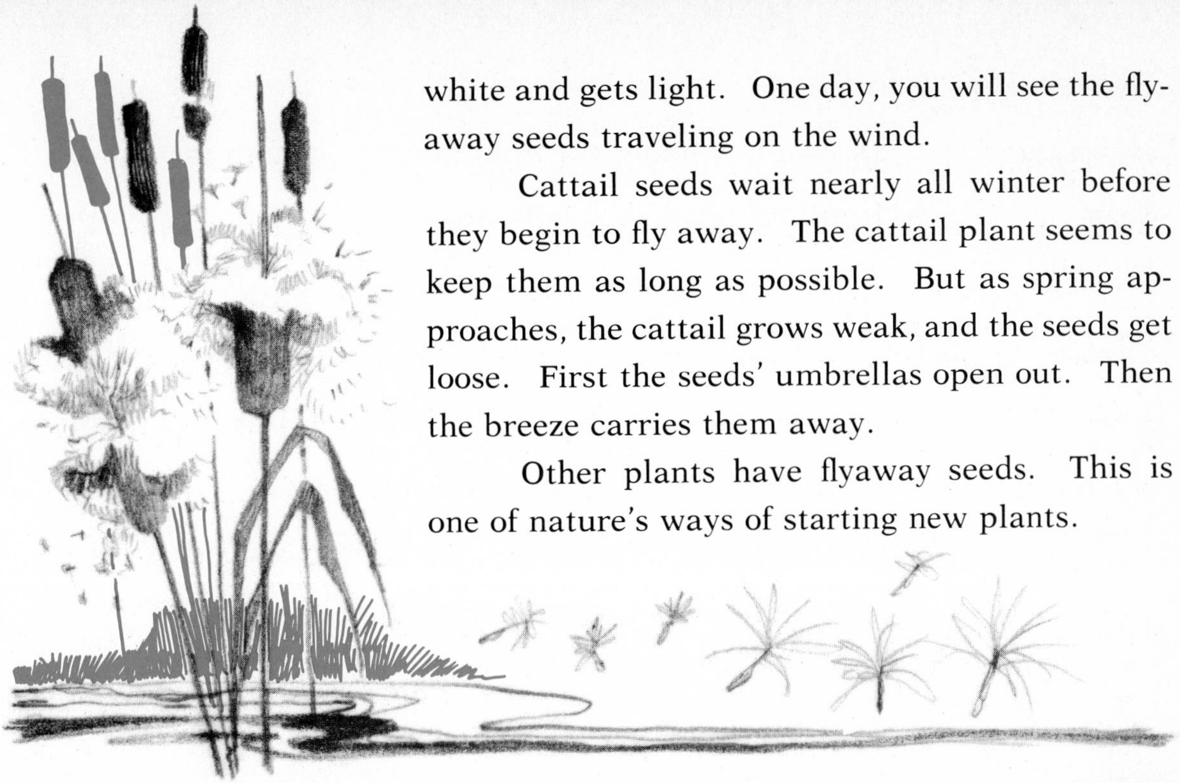

white and gets light. One day, you will see the flyaway seeds traveling on the wind.

Cattail seeds wait nearly all winter before they begin to fly away. The cattail plant seems to keep them as long as possible. But as spring approaches, the cattail grows weak, and the seeds get loose. First the seeds' umbrellas open out. Then the breeze carries them away.

Other plants have flyaway seeds. This is one of nature's ways of starting new plants.

D-5 Testing Yourself

NUMBER RIGHT

Draw a line under the right answer or fill in the blank.

1. On the end of every dandelion seed is a tiny ______________________.

2. From the story, you can tell that
   a. flyaway seeds cannot travel far without wind.
   b. cattail seeds turn white before they fly away.
   c. seeds fly away in the winter.

3. This story on the whole is about
   a. the flyaway seeds of two plants.
   b. the cattail plant.
   c. dandelion seeds.
   d. the way that all seeds travel.

4. The dandelion is the only plant with flyaway seeds.
   Yes No Does not say

5. Sunflowers have flyaway seeds. Yes No Does not say

6. What word in the last sentence means **beginning?** ______________________

Getting Ready to Read

SAY AND KNOW

churn

folk music

richness

British Isles

Scottish

bagpipes

hand-me-downs

evening

Draw a line under the right answer or fill in the blank.

1. It means **music that tells stories.** **folk music** **bagpipes** **churn**
2. It's **what you do to make butter.** **hand-me-downs** **churn** **Scottish**
3. It means the same as **wealth.** **evening** **Isles** **richness**
4. It is **a Scottish musical instrument.** **churn** **bagpipes** **Isles**
5. **The early nighttime** is **the** **bagpipes** **Scottish** **evening.**
6. **Clothes that are passed on from person to person** are ________________.

D-6 Telling Stories in Song

Many people in the Cumberland Mountains were very poor. Jean Ritchie's family wore hand-me-down clothes until they wore out. Some of Ritchie's 13 brothers and sisters didn't get shoes of their own until they were 11 years old.

The family didn't have money, but the members had something else. They had a kind of richness. It was their singing.

The whole family knew about music. Their music, called *folk music,* told stories. Songs told about the mountains and about the hard life of the workers. Songs told who was born and who died.

The mountain people Jean Ritchie knew were part of the group who had come here from the British Isles in the 1760s. Their special way of singing told where they came from. They could make their voices sound a little like the Scottish bagpipes.

The Ritchie family sang while they worked in the fields. They sang while they churned butter. They sang while they sat on the porch in the evening. Music was an important part of their lives.

D-6 Testing Yourself

NUMBER RIGHT

Draw a line under the right answer or fill in the blank.

1. Many mountain people were __________.

2. From the story, you can tell that
   a. people can be happy without being rich.
   b. big families like to work together.
   c. the mountains are very cold in winter.

3. This story as a whole is about
   a. a mountain family.
   b. churning butter.
   c. writing songs.
   d. making money.

4. The Ritchie family was large. Yes No Does not say

5. The Ritchie family liked to climb mountains. Yes No Does not say

6. What word in the third paragraph, first sentence, means **all of a thing?**

____

Getting Ready to Read

SAY AND KNOW

hundreds

subtract

humans

multiplication

computer

answers

fingers

Draw a line under the right answer or fill in the blank.

1. It means **a solution.** **a finger** **an answer** **a computer**
2. Parts of your hand are **answers** **hundreds** **fingers.**
3. It means about the same as **large numbers.** **hundreds** **answers** **subtract**
4. **People** means the same as **computers** **numbers** **humans.**
5. **A machine for doing math** is **an answer** **a counter** **a computer.**
6. If you multiply, you are doing ____________________.

D-7 The Earliest Computers

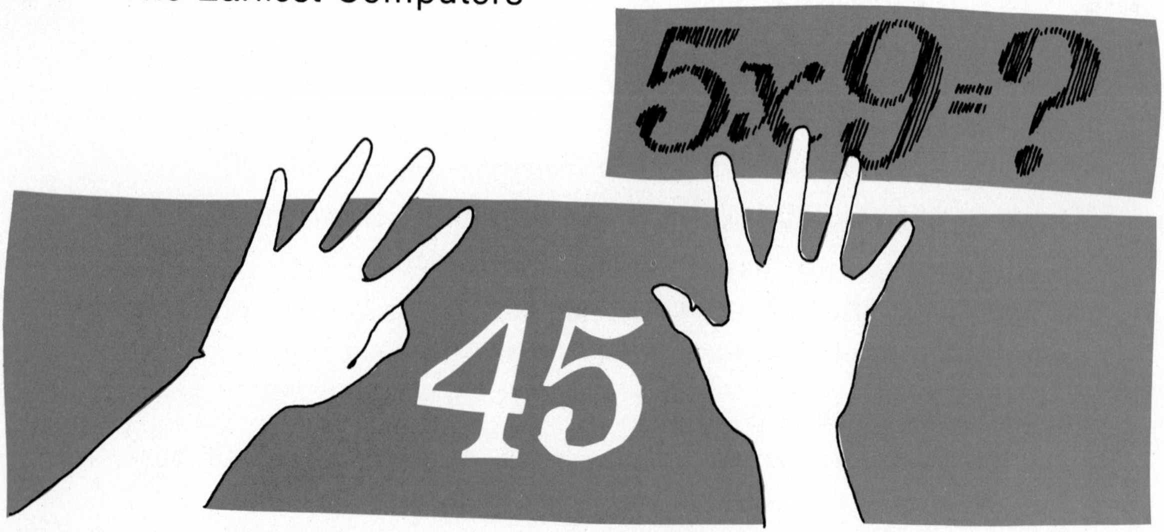

People have always had to count things. Early humans used their fingers to count. They added and subtracted with their fingers. They even did simple multiplication with their fingers. In a way, fingers were the first computers.

We can use our fingers to multiply numbers by nine. We start with the littlest finger on the left hand and give each finger a number. To find the answer to 5 × 9, find the finger that stands for 5. Bend that finger down. Now there are four fingers raised to the left of the bent finger. There are five fingers to the right of the bent finger. Putting these two numbers together gives the answer, 45.

Now try another one. Find the answer to 2 × 9. What is your answer?

You are using your fingers as a kind of computer. People have known how to multiply like this for hundreds of years.

D-7 Testing Yourself

NUMBER RIGHT ____

Draw a line under the right answer or fill in the blank.

1. People have always had to ______________ things.

2. From the story, you can tell that
  a. early people could not do math without machines.
  b. people have always found ways to do what was needed.
  c. early people invented most of the machines that we use today.

3. This story as a whole is about
  a. adding with our fingers.
  b. building computers.
  c. multiplying with fingers.
  d. early humans.

4. Fingers are like computers. Yes No Does not say

5. We can divide with our fingers. Yes No Does not say

6. What word in the last sentence means **make numbers larger?**

____

Getting Ready to Read

SAY AND KNOW
Italy
Italian
farmworkers
bowling
newcomers
immigrants
community
market
alive
lawyer

Draw a line under the right answer or fill in the blank.

1. It means **people who farm.** **market** **farmworkers** **lawyers**
2. **Someone who has just come to a place** is **an Italian** **a lawyer** **a newcomer.**
3. **Having life** is **being** **bowling** **alive** **community.**
4. **A kind of ball game** is called **alive** **market** **bowling.**
5. **One who moves to a new country** is **bowling** **a farmworker** **an immigrant.**
6. **A place to shop** is **a** ________________________.

D-8 Keeping the Old Ways

Carroll Gardens is the name of an Italian community in Brooklyn, New York. It has been a home to Italian immigrants for 100 years. Italians who live in Carroll Gardens can tell you how their life in America is different from that in Italy. In Italy, the members of a family may have been farmworkers through the years. Here, the children of such families may plan to become lawyers or

doctors. In Italy, very few in their village would have gone to college at all.

Even with their new way of life, many of the Italians want to stay in their community. They can keep the parts of their past that are important to them. People shop in meat markets and fish markets just as they do at home. Carts in the streets carry fruit and vegetables for sale.

The children like to play baseball. But the older men still play *bocce* (boch'ē). This is a kind of Italian bowling game. These Italians keep the old way of life alive. They also help newcomers learn about America.

D-8 Testing Yourself

NUMBER RIGHT

Draw a line under the right answer or fill in the blank.

1. Italian children here like to play ______________________.

2. From the story, you can tell that
   a. Italians run the best meat markets.
   b. Italians had a chance at better jobs in America.
   c. Italians like to play only baseball.

3. This story as a whole is about
   a. Italian markets.
   b. an Italian community.
   c. New York markets.
   d. Italian baseball.

4. Bocce ball is a kind of Italian game. Yes No Does not say

5. Most Italians become doctors. Yes No Does not say

6. What word in the first sentence means **a group living together?**

____

Getting Ready to Read

SAY AND KNOW

eyelids

shades

blink

eyelashes

pupil

tears

Draw a line under the right answers.

1. **Something that keeps out light** is **a** **shade** **pupil** **blink.**
2. **One part of the eye** is called **the** **blink** **eyelid** **shade.**
3. **The little brushes over the eye** are called **eyelids** **eyelashes** **blinks.**
4. **The center of the eye** is **the** **blink** **pupil** **shades.**
5. **Salty drops in the eyes** are **eyelids** **tears** **blink.**
6. **To open and close quickly** is **to** **tear** **shade** **blink.**

D-9 Watch Those Eyes

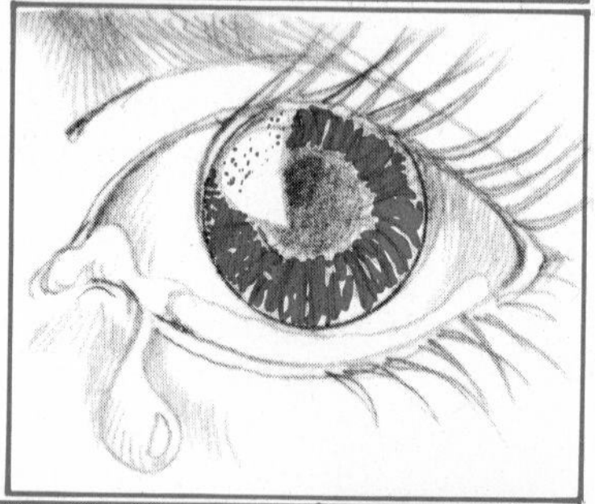

Our eyes are of great value to us. A wall of bone around each eye protects the eye. The eyelids work like little shades. As we blink, they keep out light. When we sleep, they stay closed over the eyes.

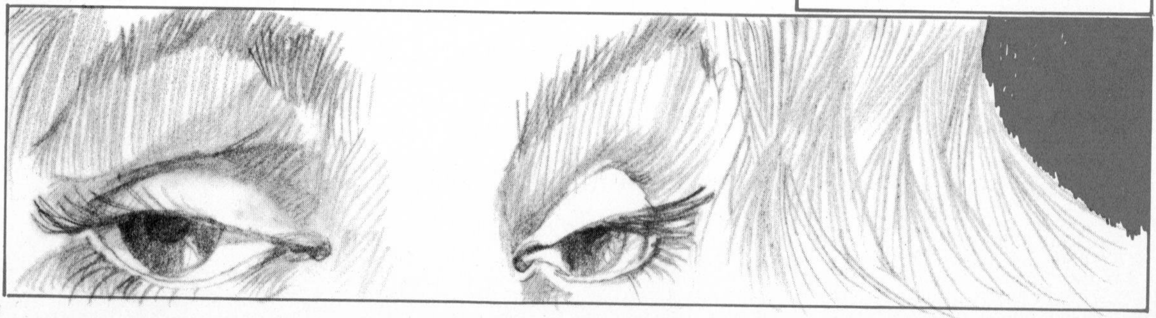

The eyelashes are like little brushes. They keep dust and other small pieces of dirt from getting into the eyes.

Tears keep the eyes warm and clean. They can help wash things out of the eye. The eyes always stay a little wet. Sometimes cold air or wind will bring more tears.

The pupil is the dark spot you see in the middle of the eye. That small hole lets the light in. When you need a lot of light to see, the pupil gets very large. Then lots of light comes into your eye. On bright sunny days, you don't need a lot of light to see. Then the pupil gets very small.

Your eye makes these changes without your even thinking about them.

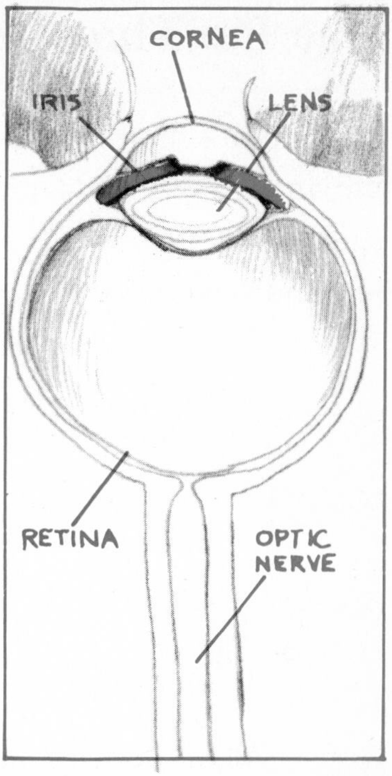

D-9 Testing Yourself

NUMBER RIGHT

Draw a line under the right answer or fill in the blank.

1. As we blink, the eyelids keep out ______________________.

2. From the story, you can tell that
   a. many parts work to protect our eyes.
   b. cold air may be bad for the eyes.
   c. large pupils are bad for the eyes.

3. This story as a whole is about
   a. how parts of our eyes work.
   b. reading on sunny days.
   c. taking good care of our eyes.
   d. the best light for cleaning.

4. The pupil lets light into the eye. Yes No Does not say

5. On bright days, sunglasses work best. Yes No Does not say

6. What word in the first sentence means **worth?** ______________________

The Pie That Grew

Bob's mother packed an apple pie in a box. "It's too bad," she said, "that Mr. Lewis has lost his job and his wife is ill. That family may be facing a grim Thanksgiving day. Take your bike, Bob, and carry this over to them. Send them my regards."

Bob tied the box to the handlebars of his bicycle and started off. On the way, he met his friend Jan.

"What do you have in that box, Bob?" she asked.

"An apple pie for the Lewises," he said.

"Wait just a moment," said Jan. She ran into the house and came out with another box. "Here is some molasses candy that Tim and I just made!" she said. "Take it to the Lewises with your pie."

Bob tied the second box to his bicycle and started on. He was in such a hurry that he almost ran into his grandmother.

"Where are you going with those boxes, Robert?" she asked.

"I am taking a pie and some molasses candy to the Lewises for their Thanksgiving dinner," Bob said.

"They will need more than that," said Grandmother. She got a basket of tea, sugar, and potatoes. "It isn't much," she said, "but it will keep the pie company."

Bob hung the basket on the handlebars of his bicycle and went on. He had not gone far when he met an old gentleman with his arms full of packages. "Where are you going in such a hurry?" asked the old gentleman.

"I am taking a pie, some molasses candy, and a basket of tea, sugar, and potatoes to the Lewises sir," Bob explained. "They are for Thanksgiving dinner."

The gentleman asked, "Could you manage to tie this bag of oranges to your bicycle seat?"

Bob could and did. There seemed to be some kind of magic in the little apple pie. As Bob passed the butcher's shop, the butcher himself said, "What are all those bundles?"

"A pie, some molasses candy, tea, sugar, potatoes, and oranges for the Lewises' Thanksgiving dinner," answered Bob.

"What, no chicken?" asked the butcher. He went into his shop and brought out a fine roasting chicken in a bag. "Can you tie this on, too?" he asked. "Perhaps they can use it."

Indeed Bob could! He raced off to the Lewises' house. The apple pie had grown into a whole dinner, from chicken to dessert. Most kind deeds do grow into something larger and better.

Carolyn Sherwin Bailey

MY READING TIME _______ (410 WORDS)

Thinking It Over

1. Why do you think that Bob's mother did not send a whole dinner?

2. What made the others feel like adding to the meal?

3. Why do kind deeds grow?

Getting Ready to Read

SAY AND KNOW

electricity
nuclear
collector
rays
motor
energy
invention
power
mirror
modern
reflected
orbit

Draw a line under the right answer or fill in the blank.

1. Light that is thrown back is **nuclear** **modern** **reflected.**
2. This means **energy to move something.** **rays** **mirror** **power**
3. **One form of energy** is **collector** **motor** **electricity.**
4. It means **the path around a planet.** **rays** **mirror** **orbit**
5. **The sun's beams** are its **mirror** **motor** **rays.**
6. What word means **something that people create?** ______________________

E-1 New Kinds of Power

In the past, we have used animals, water, and wind to give us power. Today, we use also steam, fuel, electricity, and nuclear energy.

We are also finding ways to use the sun for energy. Many modern inventions are set up with mirrors to catch the sun's rays. The rays are then

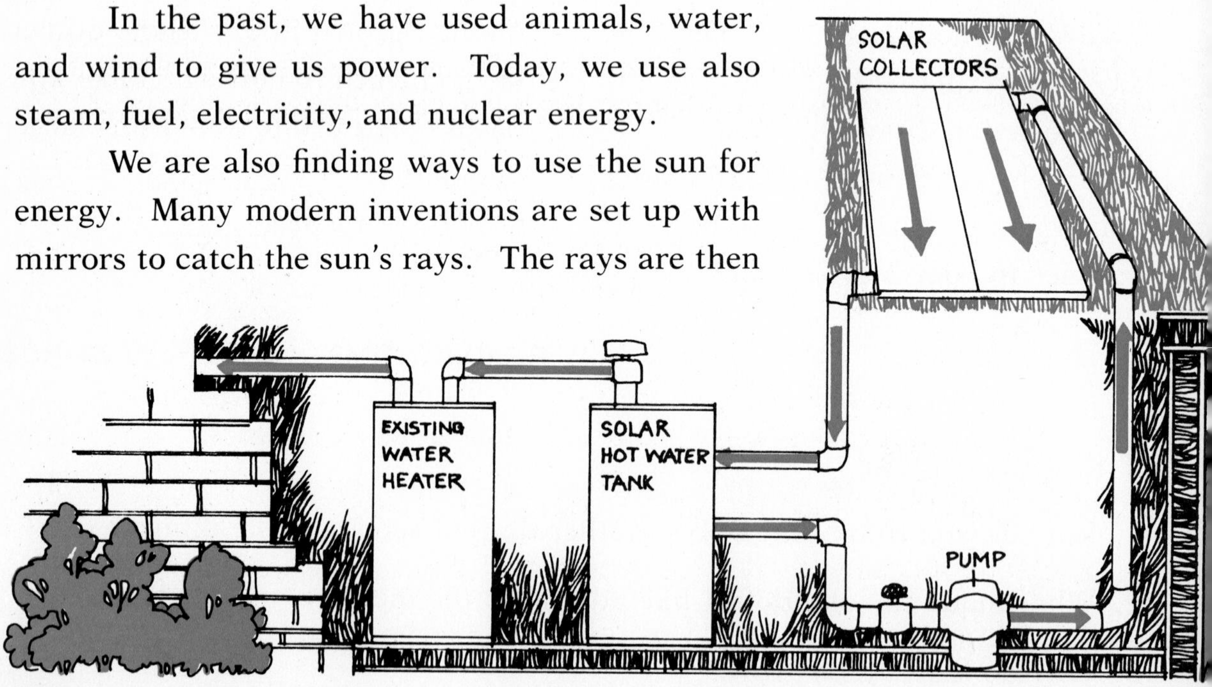

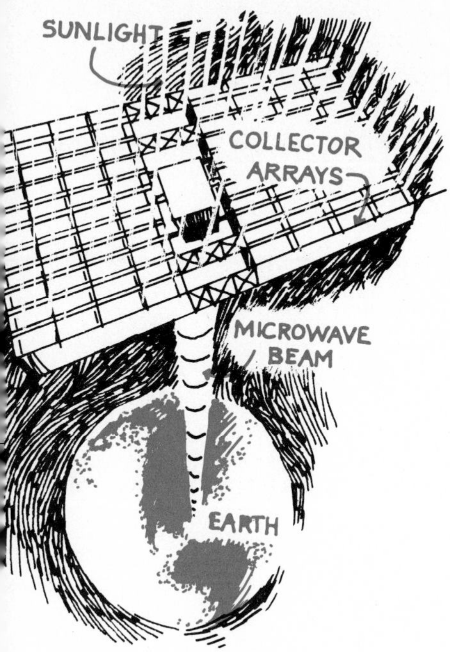

reflected to one place. They create energy that may be used to power engines. One of these inventions is no larger than a safety pin. It uses a tiny mirror to reflect the sunlight. The new unit can provide enough power to light a small light bulb.

Another method puts a heat collector in space. As the collector rides in orbit, it reflects the sun's rays back to Earth.

Many people are coming up with their own inventions for using sun power. One person used the sun to heat plastic bags filled with water. At night, special doors on the roof closed over the bags to keep in the collected heat to warm the house.

E-1 Testing Yourself

NUMBER RIGHT

Draw a line under the right answer or fill in the blank.

1. We have used animals, water, and wind to give us __________.

2. From the story, you can tell that
- a. there are many ways to collect the sun's energy.
- b. there is one sure way to use the sun's energy.
- c. people have always used the sun's energy.

3. This story as a whole is about
- a. new kinds of energy.
- b. heating with electricity.
- c. electric inventions.
- d. using light bulbs.

4. Heat collectors reflect the sun's rays. Yes No Does not say

5. Nuclear energy is a new form of power. Yes No Does not say

6. What word in the last sentence means **gathered?** ____________________

Getting Ready to Read

SAY AND KNOW

Arizona
New Mexico
Pueblo
warrior
flat-topped
enter
attack
consider
squash
openings

Draw a line under the right answer or fill in the blank.

1. **Holes like doors and windows** are **Pueblo** **tops** **openings.**
2. **To come in** means **to** **open** **consider** **enter.**
3. **To think about** is **to** **consider** **attack** **fight.**
4. Something with a point is not **in Arizona** **flat-topped** **a squash.**
5. **One Native American tribe** is called **Pueblo** **flat-top** **squash.**
6. **A fighter** is the same as **a** ______________.

E-2 Where Are the Doors?

A Native American tribe called the Pueblos lived in the Southwest long before the Spanish arrived in the 1500s. On flat-topped hills in Arizona and New Mexico, the tribe built homes of sun-dried brick. These adobe brick houses had no doors. They were entered through openings in the flat roofs. Ladders were used to get up to the roof. On top of one house, but set back, another house was built. Some of the Pueblo villages had several hundred people living in houses. They were built against each other and one on top of another. Each house had its ladder and roof door. In these homes, the Pueblos were safe from their enemies.

The Pueblos were farmers rather than warriors. They were good fighters, however, if they were attacked. Pueblo farmers grew corn, beans, and squashes. They also raised cotton, wove cloth, and made beautiful pottery.

Pueblo people still live in this area. Some of the same activities continue.

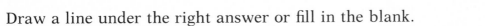

E-2 Testing Yourself

NUMBER RIGHT

Draw a line under the right answer or fill in the blank.

1. The Pueblos built houses of brick called ___________.

2. From the story, you can tell that
 a. Pueblos were not nomads.
 b. Pueblos liked war.
 c. Pueblos could not make baskets.

3. This story as a whole is about
 a. a special kind of Native American house.
 b. what the Pueblos raised.
 c. building a Pueblo village.
 d. the Sioux tribes.

4. These Native Americans raised sheep. Yes No Does not say

5. These Native Americans were a peaceful people. Yes No Does not say

6. What word in the second paragraph, last sentence, means **containers made of clay?** ____________________

Getting Ready to Read

SAY AND KNOW

clearing
remained
removed
prevent
product
erect
stump

Draw a line under the right answer or fill in the blank.

1. It means **taken away.** **remain** **removed** **stump**
2. It means **to keep from happening.** **clearing** **removed** **prevent**
3. **To build** is **to** **clear** **remain** **erect.**
4. **Something that is made or produced** is **a** **remain** **prevent** **product.**
5. It means **were left behind.** **remained** **removed** **stump**
6. What word means **an opening from which brush and trees have been taken away?** ____________________

E-3 Clearing the Forests

A pioneer family moving into new forest country first erected a cabin. Next they cleared away the trees and brush. After the trees had been removed, the field was called a *clearing*. Some tree stumps remained. The pioneers plowed the ground around them. They planted seeds as best they could. Families then raised vegetables.

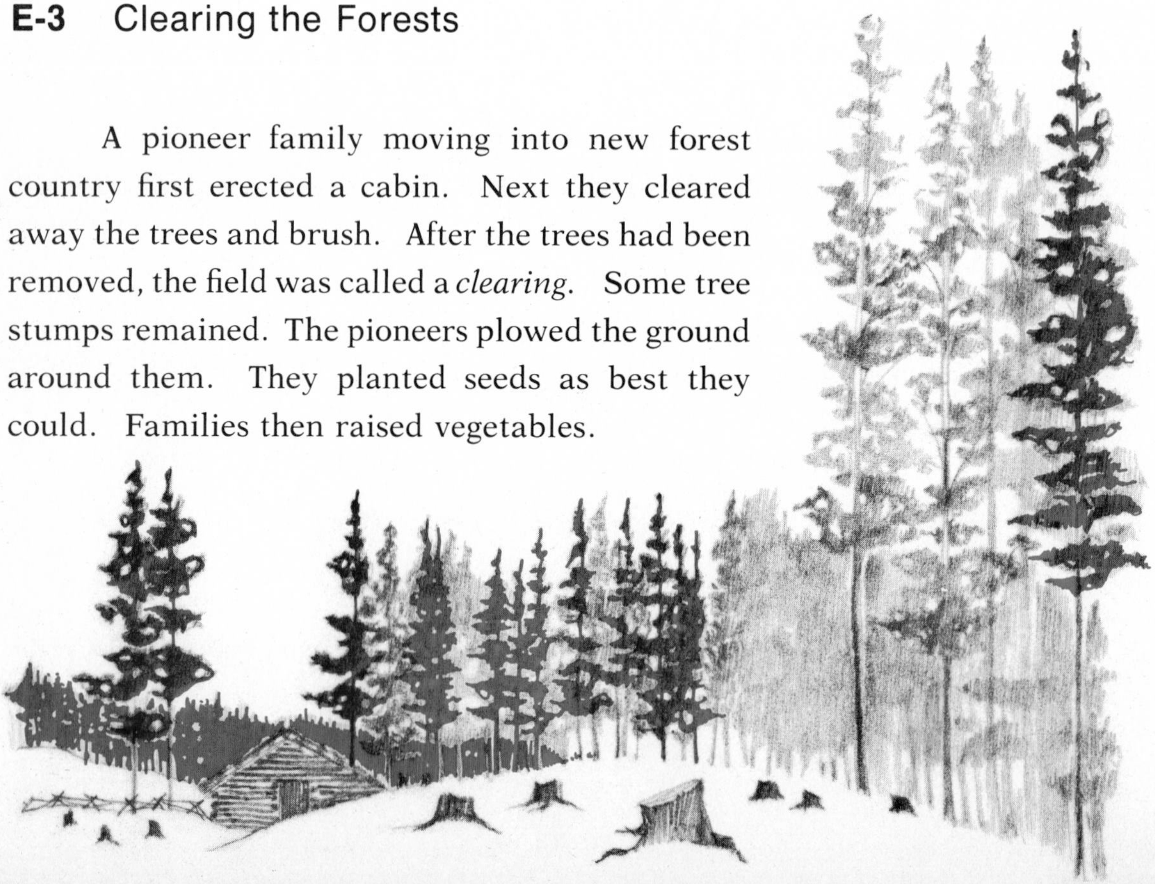

Besides their crops, the pioneers added many other things to their meals. They hunted wild game. They fished in the streams and lakes. Often, they gathered nuts, wild berries, plums, and other fruit from the woods. Certain wild plants were used as "greens." These tasted very good when cooked with fat meat.

Much forest had to be cleared to give the pioneers space. Since then, other forests have been cleared. We use the trees for paper and wood products. We use the land for houses and highways. People have begun to worry about protecting our forests. Now some areas have laws that prevent trees from being cut down.

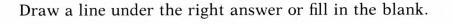

E-3 Testing Yourself

NUMBER RIGHT ____

Draw a line under the right answer or fill in the blank.

1. Pioneers used certain wild plants as ______________________.

2. From the story, you can tell that
   a. over the years, too many trees were cut down.
   b. tree stumps were good for the crops.
   c. pioneers cut down just the right number of trees.

3. This story as a whole is about
   a. the pioneers' crops and food.
   b. the pioneers' clearing.
   c. food from the store.
   d. the well-fed pioneers.

4. All pioneers were good workers. Yes No Does not say

5. Pioneers planted corn and other things. Yes No Does not say

6. What word in the second sentence means **bushes and small plants?**

____

Getting Ready to Read

SAY AND KNOW	Draw a line under the right answer or fill in the blank.
amusing	1. **Something funny** is **hollow** **common** **amusing.**
cutworm	2. It is **the opposite of largest.** **common** **elf** **tiniest**
barred	3. **Something with bars** is **Texas** **cutworm** **barred.**
hollow	4. **Something that is usual** is **Texas** **common** **hollow.**
Texas	5. It is **a state.** **cutworm** **elf** **Texas**
common	6. What word means **a tiny make-believe being or fairy?**
elf	
tiniest	______________

E-4 A Useful Bird

The owl is an amusing bird. It sleeps in the daytime and hunts for food at night. Some farmers like it because it catches mice and rats for food. It also eats grasshoppers, cutworms, and other insects. The owl swallows food whole. Later it spits up the bones, skin, and hair in little balls.

When the owl gets ready to build its nest, it gathers grass and feathers. It builds in a hollow tree trunk. Soon the nest may hold four or five eggs.

There are many kinds of owls of different sizes and colors. In the far north, we find white owls that match the white snow. On farms, we find the common brown barn owl. In Texas, we find the tiniest owl of all, called the *elf owl.*

Birds like the owl lose their homes when forests are cut down. Some people are now working to pass laws to protect these important birds.

E-4 Testing Yourself

NUMBER RIGHT

Draw a line under the right answer or fill in the blank.

1. The owl hunts for food at __________.

2. From the story, you can tell that
   a. owls living in the forest are all large.
   b. owls of today live in the desert.
   c. owls do an important job for farmers.

3. This story as a whole is about
   a. groups that kill owls.
   b. the life of owls.
   c. the white owl of the far north.
   d. a bird with a sad song.

4. Other birds hate owls. Yes No Does not say

5. Owls should be killed. Yes No Does not say

6. What word in the last sentence means about the same as **take care of?**

____

Getting Ready to Read

SAY AND KNOW

maple
ripen
whirl
whirling
paddle
sailaway
autumn
linger

Draw a line under the right answer or fill in the blank.

1. It is **a kind of tree.** **sailaway** **maple** **autumn**
2. It is **the name of a season.** **linger** **autumn** **paddle**
3. This means **turning around and around** or **spinning.** **whirl** **whirling** **lingering**
4. **To become full grown** is **to** **sailaway** **paddle** **ripen.**
5. It is not a tree. **maple** **paddle** **ash**
6. What word means **to stay on?** ____________________

E-5 Sailaway Seeds

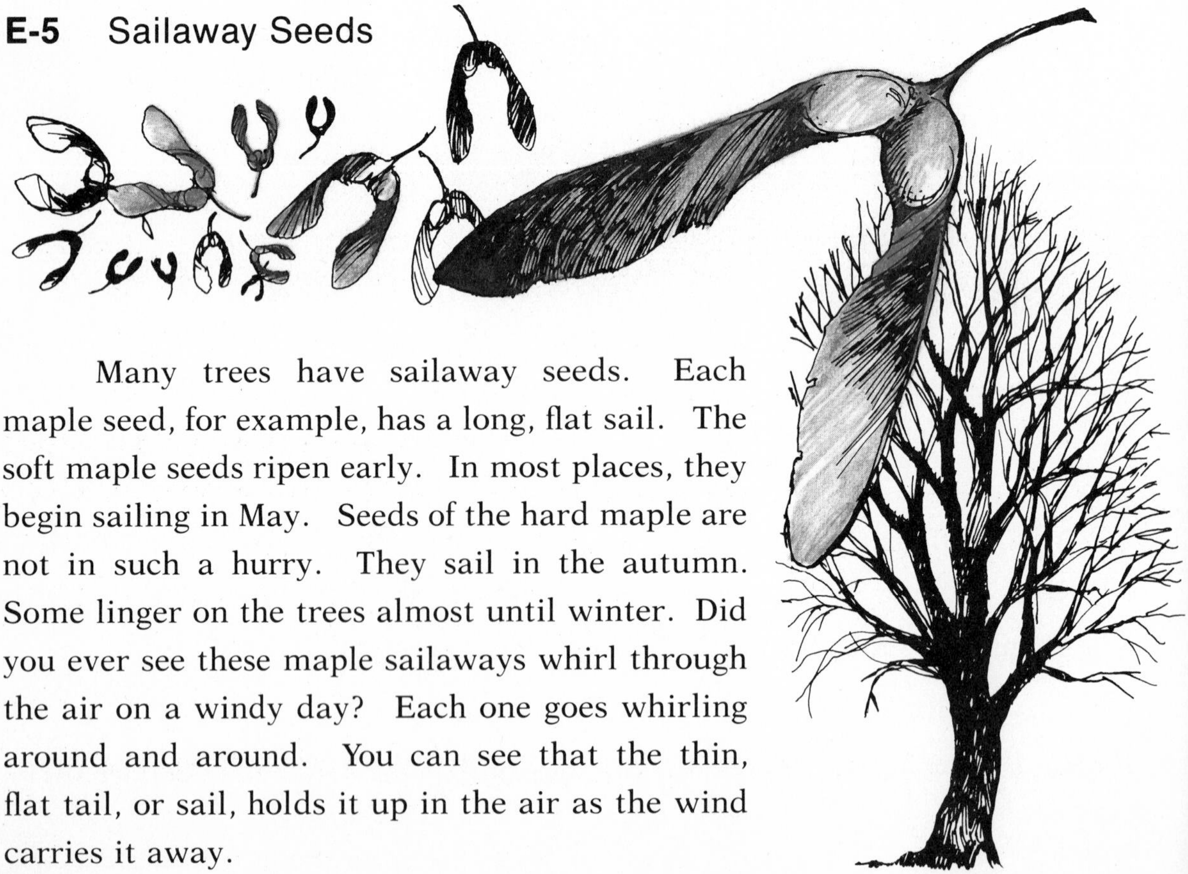

Many trees have sailaway seeds. Each maple seed, for example, has a long, flat sail. The soft maple seeds ripen early. In most places, they begin sailing in May. Seeds of the hard maple are not in such a hurry. They sail in the autumn. Some linger on the trees almost until winter. Did you ever see these maple sailaways whirl through the air on a windy day? Each one goes whirling around and around. You can see that the thin, flat tail, or sail, holds it up in the air as the wind carries it away.

The sailaway seeds of the ash tree are shaped like paddles. The handle is the seed. The sail is the flat part of the paddle. In the fall, soon after the leaves are all gone, the seeds begin to go, too. Few of them start early. They can travel best on snow and ice.

E-5 Testing Yourself

NUMBER RIGHT

Draw a line under the right answer or fill in the blank.

1. Two trees with sailaway seeds are the __________ and the __________.

2. From the story, you can tell that
   a. sailaway seeds cannot travel far on calm days.
   b. all sailaway seeds begin to travel in May.
   c. maple trees do not have seeds.

3. This story as a whole is about
   a. the seeds of all trees.
   b. maple seeds and how they travel.
   c. the seeds of ash and birch trees.
   d. the sailaway seeds of two trees.

4. Sailaway seeds travel on the wind. Yes No Does not say

5. Sailaway seeds are the fastest travelers of any seeds.
   Yes No Does not say

6. What word in the last sentence means **go from one place to another?**

   ____

Getting Ready to Read

SAY AND KNOW

shabby
products
migrant
union
boycott
marshmallow
Chicano
justice
Huerta
Chavez

Draw a line under the right answer or fill in the blank.

1. **Something very worn** is **boycott products shabby.**
2. **Fairness** means **justice migrant marshmallow.**
3. **Someone who moves from one place to another** is a **boycott migrant union.**
4. **To refuse to buy a product** is **to migrant boycott union.**
5. **A group that works for the rights of workers** is **a boycott union migrant.**
6. It is **a soft, sweet, or weak person** ______________________.

E-6 Don't Be a Marshmallow!

"Don't be a marshmallow. Work for justice." Those were the words Dolores Huerta used. She wanted people to fight for the rights of migrant workers. As a child, Dolores Huerta had worked in the fields. She knew that workers often were not treated well. They got very low pay. Their houses were very shabby.

When she grew up, Huerta and other Chicano leaders, such as Cesar Chavez, wanted to form groups called *unions*. These groups would help workers get fair rules for working and living.

When the bosses said no to the idea of unions, the leaders and the workers started a boycott. A boycott tries to stop the sale of a certain product. The workers wanted all Americans to stop buying grapes until things got better for the migrants.

In the 1970s, Huerta traveled from city to city. She fought for the rights of her people. Huerta wanted others to stand up and fight, too. That's why she said, "Don't be a marshmallow!"

E-6 Testing Yourself

NUMBER RIGHT

Draw a line under the right answer or fill in the blank.

1. Huerta had worked in the ______________________.

2. From the story, you can tell that
   a. field workers needed people to help them.
   b. field workers wanted to do things alone.
   c. field workers liked grapes best.

3. This story as a whole is about
   a. getting more money for farmers.
   b. getting products to farmers.
   c. getting fair rules for workers.
   d. traveling from city to city.

4. Huerta traveled from city to city. Yes No Does not say

5. Huerta liked to travel. Yes No Does not say

6. What word in the second sentence means **fairness?** ______________________

Getting Ready to Read

SAY AND KNOW

abacus

pointer

invention

math

communities

ancient

expert

model

counters

shopkeepers

Draw a line under the right answer or fill in the blank.

1. It means **something invented.**
an invention **an abacus** **a model**

2. A thing made to look like something else is
math **an expert** **a model.**

3. It means the same as **groups of people.**
abacus **marks** **communities**

4. Something to point with is **a pointer** **an expert** **a counter.**

5. Someone who knows a great deal about a topic is
a model **an expert** **an abacus.**

6. It means about the same as **arithmetic.** __________

E-7 The Oldest Still Works

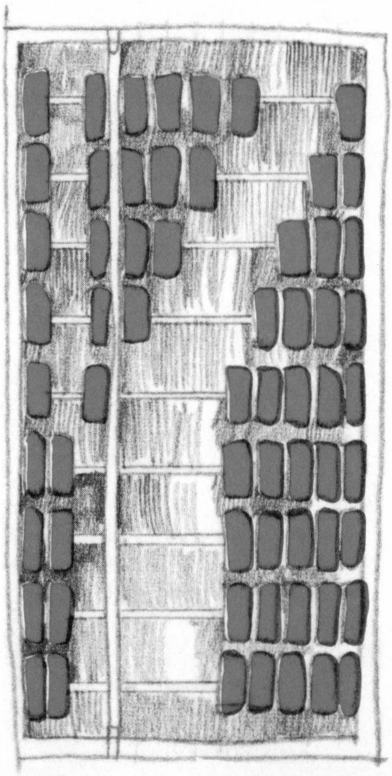

Some inventions work so well they never change. The abacus is a math tool that was invented thousands of years ago. This simple tool has hardly changed since then. It has rods with beads on them, set up to help us count.

The word *abacus* comes from the Greek word for dust. Some people think that the first abacus may have been a board. It seems that this board was covered with dust or sand. The user then put marks on the dust with a pointer.

The Chinese, Japanese, and Romans all used a kind of abacus. The Chinese abacus was used about 3000 years ago. In Chinese communities,

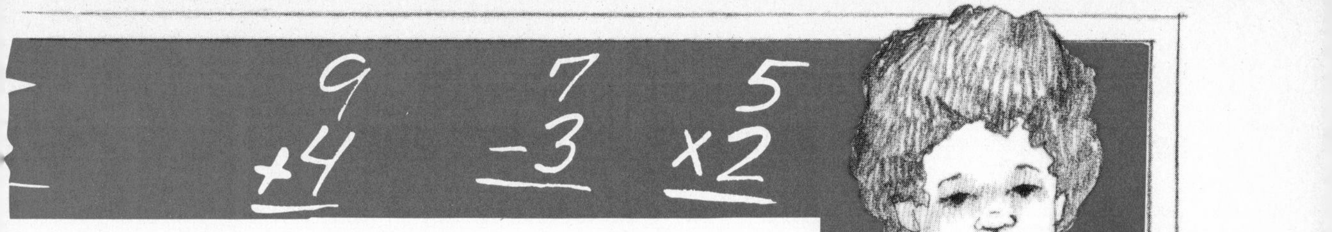

you can still see shopkeepers using this tool. In the hands of an expert, it can be as fast as an electric calculator!

In classrooms today, children are using the abacus to learn about place value to count in units of tens. They make their own models, using beads or beans as the counters. This ancient tool still works for them, too.

E-7 Testing Yourself

NUMBER RIGHT ______

Draw a line under the right answer or fill in the blank.

1. Some inventions never ______________________.

2. From the story, you can tell that
   a. using an abacus is easy.
   b. an abacus was not an important tool.
   c. numbers have always been important.

3. This story as a whole is about
   a. a tool called a board.
   b. a tool called an abacus.
   c. how Romans spell.
   d. Greek tools.

4. *Abacus* comes from a Greek word. Yes No Does not say

5. The abacus is very old. Yes No Does not say

6. What word in the fourth paragraph, second sentence, means **things to count with?** ______________________

Getting Ready to Read

SAY AND KNOW

arrive
freedom
mine
treat
newcomers
immigrants
weavers
reason
China
Chinese

Draw a line under the right answer or fill in the blank.

1. **To act toward** is **to** **reason** **treat** **arrive.**
2. **Someone who weaves** is **a weaver** **an immigrant** **a mine.**
3. **The cause** means the same as **the** **reason** **freedom** **treat.**
4. **People who make their home in a new land** are **mines** **weavers** **immigrants.**
5. **To come to a place** is **to** **treat** **arrive** **mine.**
6. People from China are ______________________.

E-8 Looking for Freedom

Newcomers chose America as their home for many reasons. Some came looking for freedom. Others were brought over as slaves. They did not choose to come.

Many immigrants wanted to find the kind of work they had done at home. Maybe they had been weavers or farmers. But if they could find no other work, they went into the factories or down into the mines. Some worked at building the railroads.

Many came here because they were told wonderful stories. Between 1850 and 1882, 300,000 Chinese immigrants arrived. They had read signs in China. The signs had said, "Great pay! Get rich! Come to America!"

These signs were not telling the real story. Businesses in the United States wanted cheap workers. They did not really want to pay well. They did not want to help the Chinese get rich. The Chinese were often treated very badly when they did arrive.

Although newcomers like the Chinese were good people and hard workers, many were not happy in their new homes. It took many years to solve their problems in their new land.

E-8 Testing Yourself

NUMBER RIGHT

Draw a line under the right answer or fill in the blank.

1. Some newcomers came to America looking for ____________________.

2. From the story, you can tell that
   a. for many, the new life was no easier than the old one.
   b. most immigrants found a happy, safe life.
   c. the new life in America brought enough money for all.

3. This story as a whole is about
   a. immigrants like the Chinese.
   b. people who worked in mines.
   c. business in China.
   d. how newcomers solved problems.

4. All the Chinese got rich. Yes No Does not say

5. The Chinese worked in mines. Yes No Does not say

6. What word in the last sentence means **difficulties?** ____________________

Getting Ready to Read

SAY AND KNOW

ivy
oil
laundry
avoid
scratching
section
jewelweed
fern
cure
soothe

Draw a line under the right answers or fill in the blank.

1. It is **a climbing plant.** **ivy** **laundry** **oil**
2. Which two are plants? **jewelweed** **grows** **fern**
3. **To keep away from** means **to** **avoid** **oil** **poison.**
4. **The opposite of sickness** is **fern** **oak** **cure.**
5. What word means **part?** **strong** **section** **contact**
6. **Rubbing to stop itching** is called ______________________.

E-9 Poisons in the Woods

Poison ivy and poison oak grow in many sections of our country. There is a great deal of poison oak found on the West Coast. It is found in the southern and central states as well.

On the leaves of both plants is an oil that contains the poison. If part of your body touches the plants, the oil sticks to your skin. The poison makes your skin itch. Sometimes, just the smoke from a burning plant can bother you.

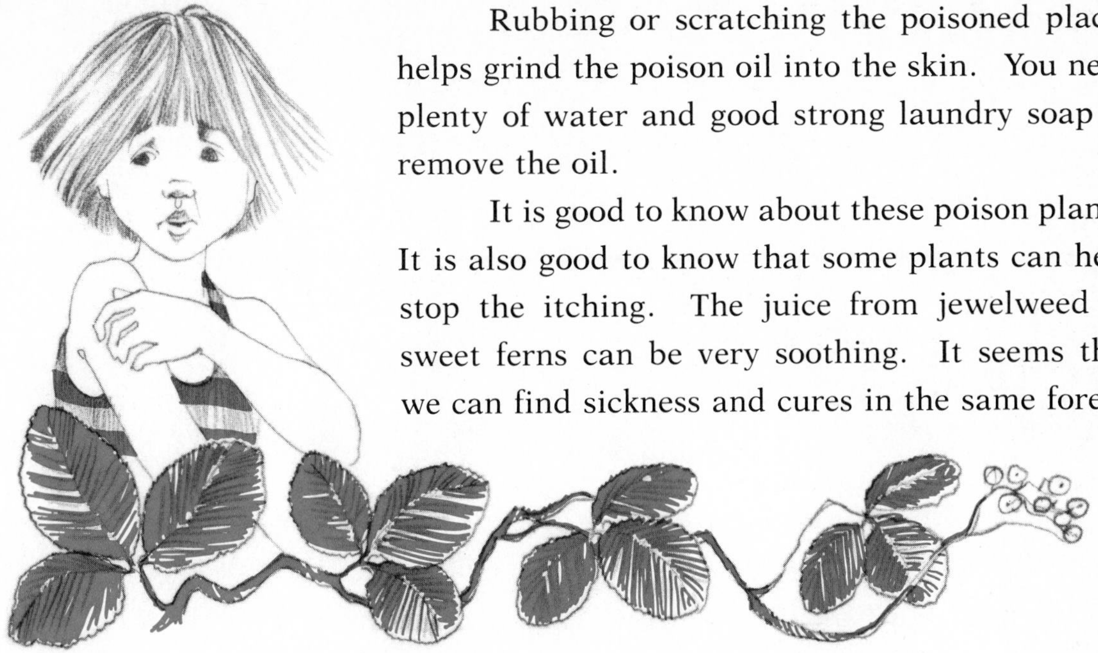

Rubbing or scratching the poisoned places helps grind the poison oil into the skin. You need plenty of water and good strong laundry soap to remove the oil.

It is good to know about these poison plants. It is also good to know that some plants can help stop the itching. The juice from jewelweed or sweet ferns can be very soothing. It seems that we can find sickness and cures in the same forest!

E-9 Testing Yourself

NUMBER RIGHT

Draw a line under the right answer or fill in the blank.

1. Plants such as sweet ferns can be ______________________.

2. From the story, you can tell that
   a. it is best not to scratch itching skin.
   b. nothing can get poison ivy oil off the skin.
   c. poison oak and poison ivy look just alike.

3. This story as a whole is about
   a. what to do if you get poisoned.
   b. what to do if your skin itches.
   c. poison ivy and poison oak.
   d. knowing a poison plant.

4. One should avoid poison plants. Yes No Does not say

5. On the West Coast, there is poison ivy. Yes No Does not say

6. What word in the second paragraph, second sentence, means about the same as **clings** or **attaches?** ______________________

Manstin Changes Moccasins

Manstin, a young Dakota brave, was alone in the woods. He came upon a house far from the town. He lifted the door flap and entered. A blind old man sat upon the ground. He was old enough to be grandfather to any living thing. When he heard Manstin enter, he said, "I cannot see you, Grandchild. Tell me your name."

"I am Manstin, Grandfather," the man answered, stepping closer. "Tell me, what is in those buckskin bags?"

"Those are magic bags," answered the grandfather. "They are filled with food, and they never grow empty." Then the old man pulled a rope that lay on his right. "This rope takes me to a brook," he said. He pulled a rope on his left. "This rope leads me to the woods."

"Grandfather!" cried Manstin. "How I wish I could live such an easy life! I would gladly give you my eyes for your place."

"All right," said the old man, "take out your eyes and give them to me. Then take my place."

Manstin took out his eyes. The old man put them in and went off. Manstin sat down to enjoy his easy life. Soon he felt thirsty. Holding one of the ropes, he went to the brook. He was impatient. In his hurry, he slipped and fell into the water. Manstin splashed about, feeling for the shore. Finally, he was able to get out. Very tired, he crawled back to the house.

Manstin was wet. His teeth chattered. The night air was cold, but he had no wood for a fire. Taking hold of the other rope, he fol-

lowed it to the woods. There Manstin gathered wood. As he did this, he let the rope go. Without a guide, the blind brave was lost. He stumbled about. He dropped his wood. He fell into a thicket. He lay groaning, unable to move.

Finally, he heard someone coming. It was the grandfather. "Here, Manstin," said the old man, "take back your eyes. I knew you would not be happy in my place."

"I have learned my lesson," said Manstin.

"I have learned mine, too," said the grandfather. "I enjoyed seeing with your young eyes, but I am too old to wander all about. I would much rather sit in my house."

The grandfather returned to his house. Manstin put his eyes back into his head and went happily on his way.

MY READING TIME ______ (410 WORDS)

Thinking It Over

1. What did Manstin learn?

2. What problems might the old man have had while using Manstin's eyes?

3. There is a saying, "Don't judge people until you have walked in their moccasins." How does this apply to the story?

Getting Ready to Read

SAY AND KNOW

deliver
stagecoach
passenger
sort
computers
spanned
speediest
carrier
modern
major

Draw a line under the right answer or fill in the blank.

1. It means **fastest.** **speediest** **carrier** **modern**
2. **Someone who pays a fare to ride on something** is a **major** **stagecoach** **passenger.**
3. **Stretched over** means **speediest** **deliver** **spanned.**
4. **Someone or something that carries** is a **carrier** **computer** **major.**
5. It means **of today.** **spanned** **modern** **stagecoach**
6. **Machines that figure problems** are ______________.

F-1 The Mail Must Go Through

Did you get a letter in the mail yesterday? In the early days of this country, people were happy to get a letter once a year. A letter was carried by riders over very poor roads. Later, stagecoaches carried the mail, as well as passengers. It took a stagecoach 24 hours to go 160 kilometers (100 miles). Today, an automobile can go that far in 2 hours.

The Pony Express riders carried mail from Missouri to California. They traveled faster than the stagecoaches. They changed ponies every 80

kilometers (50 miles). They might cover 400 kilometers (250 miles) in a day.

Finally, the railroads spanned the United States. Clerks sorted the letters in the mail cars as the train sped along. Now most mail is carried by plane to major cities. This modern mail carrier can take the mail across the country in a few hours. Computers and machines sort the mail in large sorting rooms. There, mail trucks pick it up and bring it to your neighborhood. Then mail carriers deliver it to you.

F-1 Testing Yourself

NUMBER RIGHT

Draw a line under the right answer or fill in the blank.

1. Once, the mail was carried by riders and ______________________.

2. From the story, you can tell that
   a. Pony Express riders did not carry mail from the East Coast to Missouri.
   b. today, all mail is carried by trains.
   c. people long ago did not write many letters.

3. This story as a whole is about
   a. early mail carriers.
   b. carrying the mail by airplanes.
   c. stagecoaches.
   d. carrying the mail.

4. Pony Express riders traveled faster than stagecoaches.
Yes   No   Does not say

5. Airplanes can go more than twice as fast as the fastest trains.
Yes   No   Does not say

6. What word in the last sentence means the same as **take** or **carry?**

____

Getting Ready to Read

SAY AND KNOW

smoke
raising
potato
cultivated
Spanish
explorer
contributed
world
seaweed
clams
maize

Draw a line under the right answer.

1. People from Spain are **English** **Spanish** **known.**
2. **To give** is **to** **cultivate** **explore** **contribute.**
3. **A plant that grows in the sea** is **smoke** **potato** **seaweed.**
4. It is **a starch food.** **potato** **smoke** **clams**
5. **Land used to raise crops** is **Spanish** **contributed** **cultivated.**

F-2 New Worlds, New Foods

The potato was unknown to the Europeans until they came to the New World. Spanish explorers found some of the Native South Americans cultivating potatoes. The potato is one of the things that the South Americans contributed to the world.

Tobacco also was not known to the settlers when they came to America. Explorers came from England to what is now Virginia. There, they learned from the Native Americans to use tobacco.

Another food raised by Native Americans that was strange to the settlers was called *Indian corn* or *maize.* Today, corn is grown in nearly all parts of our country.

New England women learned new ways to cook food from Native Americans. One special dish was made with clams, corn, and seaweed.

These foods were cooked in a pit in the ground. The pit was lined with rocks. Then food was placed in the pit in layers. The lid of the pit was a piece of hide.

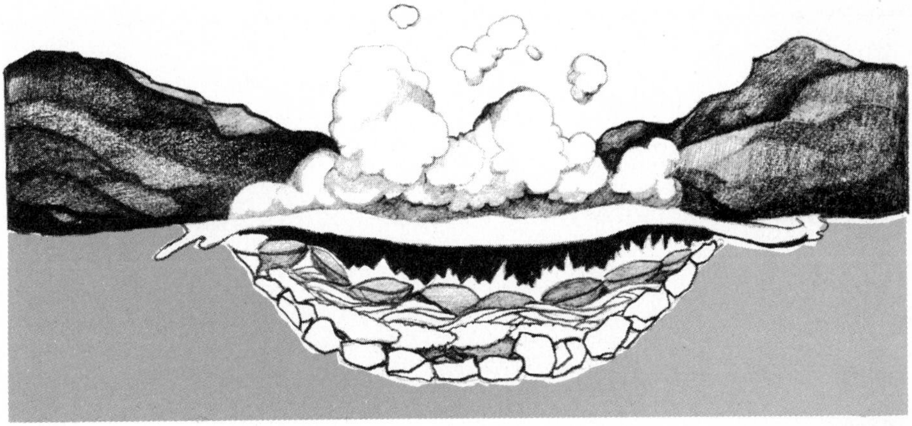

F-2 Testing Yourself

NUMBER RIGHT

Draw a line under the right answer or fill in the blank.

1. Native Americans gave the settlers potatoes, tobacco, and ___________.

2. From the story, you can tell that

- a. the Spanish settled in what is now Virginia.
- b. in very early times, people in Europe did not eat corn.
- c. Native People of North America raised potatoes.

3. This story as a whole is about

- a. Native Americans and settlers.
- b. Native American names.
- c. five plants first found in America.
- d. things the Native Americans gave the settlers.

4. Corn is grown only in the United States. Yes No Does not say

5. New England women liked to cook. Yes No Does not say

6. What word in the first sentence means **not known?** ___________

Getting Ready to Read

SAY AND KNOW

lye
grease
mixture
barrel
spout
seeps
seeped
liquid
thickened

Draw a line under the right answer or fill in the blank.

1. **A tube to carry off liquid** is **a** **mixture** **spout** **barrel.**
2. **A tall wooden tube-shaped vessel** is **a** **barrel** **grease** **lye.**
3. Liquid that moves slowly through something thick **seeps** **spouts** **barrels.**
4. This means **gotten thick.** **mixture** **thickened** **lye**
5. **Something that has been mixed** is **a** ____________________.

F-3 Making Soap for a Year

In pioneer days, soap was made at home. First the pioneers put a spout into a hole in a barrel. They placed the barrel on a bench with the spout pointing into a wooden pail. They filled the barrel with wood ashes they had saved. Then they poured water over the ashes.

The water seeped through the ashes. It came out of the spout and dropped into the pail. By then it had become a brown liquid called *lye.*

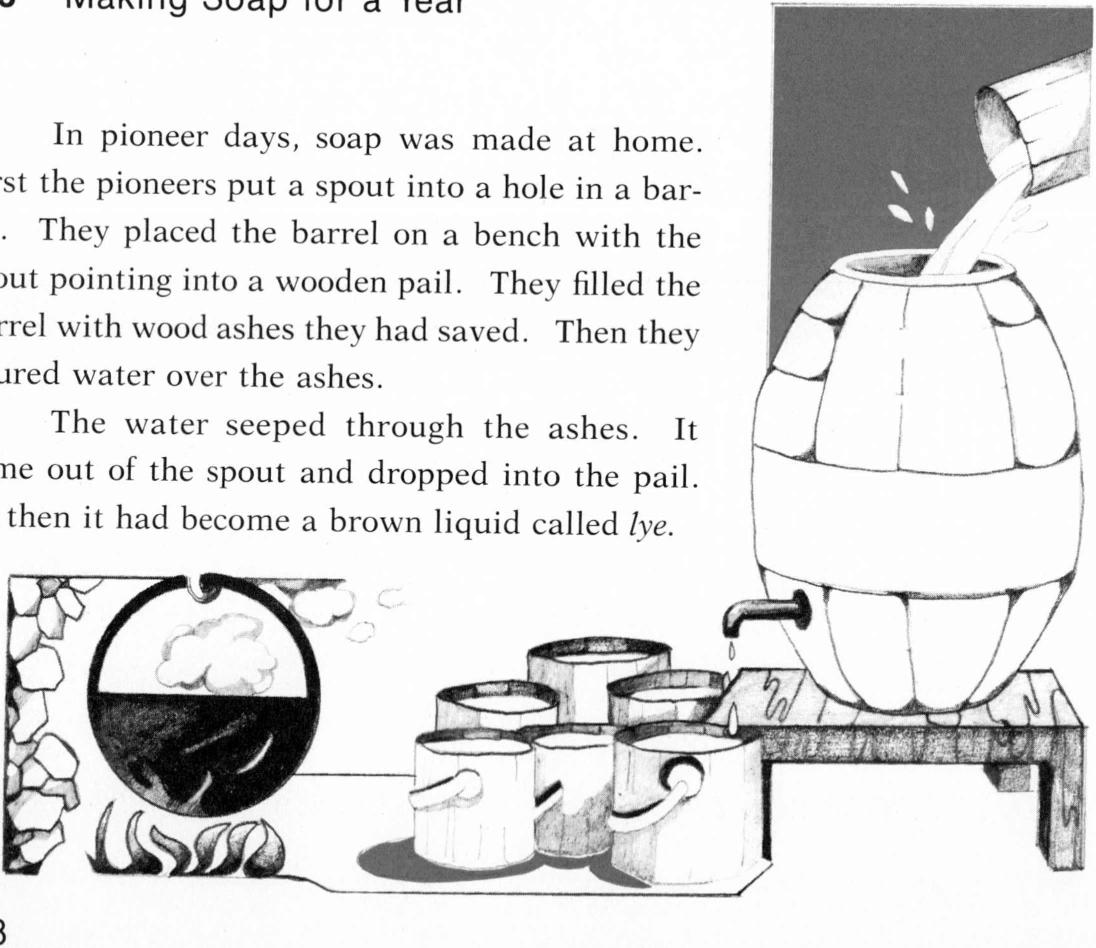

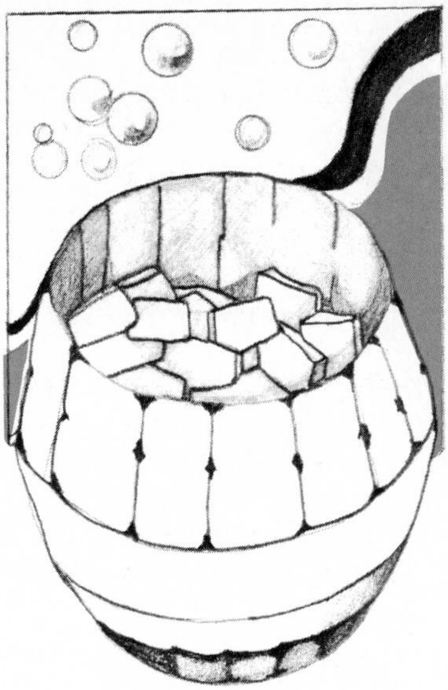

It was very important to know just how strong to make the lye. In a big kettle, grease and fat were mixed with the lye. This mixture was heated slowly for some time. When the mixture was thick enough, the kettle was cooled. The thickened lye and grease was now soap. It was kept in a barrel.

Every spring, each family made enough of this soft, yellow soap to last for a whole year. There were no books or records telling how to make soap. Many families found their own special way to do it. Then they passed on their family secret, usually from mother to daughter.

F-3 Testing Yourself

NUMBER RIGHT

Draw a line under the right answer or fill in the blank.

1. The pioneers made their soap at ______________________.
2. From the story, you can tell that
   a. pioneers did not use soap.
   b. pioneers would not waste soap.
   c. lye poured over ashes makes soap.
3. This story as a whole is about
   a. the way pioneers made soap.
   b. things needed to make soap.
   c. how the pioneers kept clean.
   d. the pioneers' work.
4. The soap made by the pioneers was hard. Yes No Does not say
5. Pioneers' soap was better than the soap we buy. Yes No Does not say
6. What word in the third sentence means **something shaped like an open drum?** ______________________

Getting Ready to Read

SAY AND KNOW	Draw a line under the right answer or fill in the blank.
ugly	**1.** It means **the opposite of beautiful.** **pleasing** **ugly** **wart**
handling	**2.** It means **believing in magic things.** **flash** **superstitious** **afraid**
superstitious	**3. Touching** or **holding** means **ugly** **studied** **handling.**
mosquito	**4. A lump on the skin** may be **a** **wart** **handling** **flash.**
flash	**5. A very brief time** is **a** **flash** **wart** **mosquito.**
wart	**6.** Which word means **a bug that bites?** ________________

F-4 Bug Catchers

At first, a toad may look ugly to you. But toads are fun to watch. You can become fond of a toad and may even think it looks good. Toads have bumpy skin. Some superstitious persons think people can get warts from handling toads. That is not true. You need not be afraid of toads, for they will not harm you.

Toads catch mosquitoes and other insects for food. They are very fond of cutworms, which harm plants in the garden. One person studied toads for a long time, watching them day after day. They ate 83 different kinds of insects. Many of these bugs are harmful to plants.

A toad catches an insect with its sticky tongue. Quick as a flash, it puts out its tongue, and the bug is caught.

Like all other animals, toads have enemies. They learn to be very careful.

F-4 Testing Yourself

NUMBER RIGHT

Draw a line under the right answer or fill in the blank.

1. On the toad's tongue is something that is ________________.

2. From the story, you can tell that
   a. toads catch insects with their sticky tails.
   b. toads have no enemies.
   c. a toad can be helpful in a garden.

3. This story as a whole is about
   a. staying away from toads.
   b. keeping toads for pets.
   c. catching toads.
   d. toads and what they eat.

4. Toads catch only insects that harm plants. Yes No Does not say

5. People can get warts from toads. Yes No Does not say

6. What word in the first paragraph, fifth sentence, means **small lumps on the skin?** ____________

Getting Ready to Read

SAY AND KNOW

springboard
prettiest
print
teacup
ripe
escape
pod
raindrops
usually
stalk

Draw a line under the right answer or fill in the blank.

1. **To get away** means **to** **print** **springboard** **escape.**
2. If fruit is ready to eat, it is **stalk** **teacup** **ripe.**
3. It means **the most pretty.** **print** **prettiest** **usually**
4. **The case in which some plants grow their seeds** is **a** **pod** **stalk** **teacup.**
5. **Most of the time** means **escape** **usually** **prettiest.**
6. It means **the stem of a plant.** ______________________

F-5 Springboard Seeds

Have you ever jumped from a springboard? Some plants furnish a springboard so their seeds can travel by jumping. Most of these seeds grow in cuplike pods. One of the prettiest plants that acts as a springboard is the butter print.

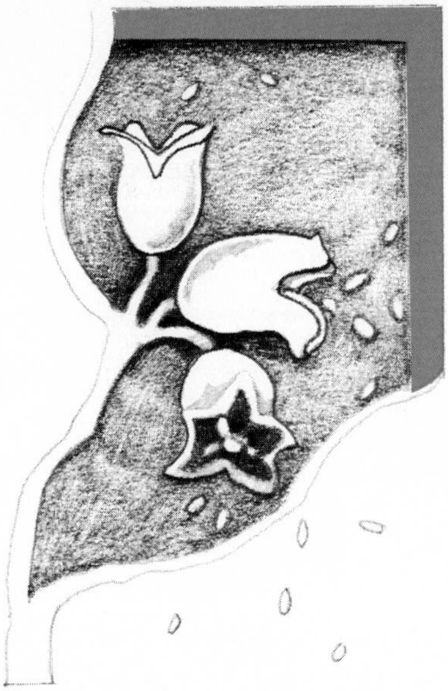

The stalk of the butter print grows 4 or 5 feet high. A butter print usually has several pods. Each one is full of little black seeds. Each pod is shaped like a wide teacup. When the seeds are ripe, they can escape through holes in the top of the pod. Then something makes the stalk or branch act like a springboard.

Just run against such a stalk sometime in October. Bend the stalk to one side, and then let it go suddenly. You will see seeds jumping through the air. They will fall like a shower of raindrops.

F-5 Testing Yourself

NUMBER RIGHT

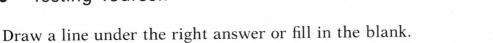

Draw a line under the right answer or fill in the blank.

1. The springboard seeds travel by ________________.

2. From the story, you can tell that
   a. springboard seeds do not travel.
   b. a number of plants have springboard seeds.
   c. the butter print is a tree.

3. This story as a whole is about
   a. butter seeds.
   b. a shower of raindrops.
   c. springboard jumping seeds.
   d. traveling by jumping.

4. The wind helps springboard seeds to travel. Yes No Does not say

5. Only one plant, called the butter print, has springboard seeds.
   Yes No Does not say

6. What word in the last sentence means **fall of rain?** ________________

Getting Ready to Read

SAY AND KNOW

viewing
comet
special
telescope
scientist
medal
discovery
excellent
Denmark
professor

Draw a line under the right answer or fill in the blank.

1. **Something unusual** is **telescope** **special** **discovery.**
2. You can view the stars with a **telescope** **medal** **comet.**
3. **Someone who studies science** is a **member** **scientist** **telescope.**
4. **Something very fine** is **medal** **comet** **excellent.**
5. **Looking at something** is **discovery** **special** **viewing.**
6. **A thing discovered** is a ______________________.

F-6 Eyes on the Stars

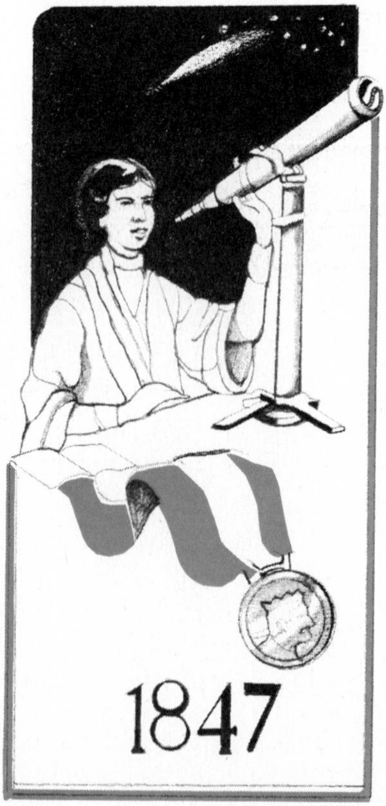

If you had been a child in the 1800s, as Maria Mitchell was, your day would have started before six o'clock. Your work and your studies might have gone on for 16 hours.

As she was growing up, Maria Mitchell loved watching the stars. On clear nights, she watched the skies through her father's telescope. Then, one night, she saw something special—a comet.

Her father wrote to a professor to tell him of the discovery. Others across the world had seen the comet, too. But Maria Mitchell was the first. She received a gold medal from the King of Denmark for her discovery. She soon became the first woman to be asked to join an important group of scientists.

Maria Mitchell had a secret thought about why women made excellent astronomers. She thought it was because of their sewing! In those times, girls like Maria were trained to sew small, fine stitches. She believed this training gave them eyes for viewing the stars. If this is so, why do you think most astronomers were men?

F-6 Testing Yourself

NUMBER RIGHT

Draw a line under the right answer or fill in the blank.

1. Maria Mitchell was a child in the ______________________.

2. From the story, you can tell that
   a. Maria Mitchell could not read well.
   b. Maria Mitchell's childhood was spent in Denmark.
   c. Maria Mitchell's father was interested in the stars, too.

3. This story as a whole is about
   a. how to see a comet.
   b. working all day.
   c. buying telescopes.
   d. a young astronomer.

4. Comets are easily seen by telescope. Yes No Does not say

5. Maria Mitchell received a silver medal from the king.
   Yes No Does not say

6. What word in the fourth sentence means **tool for seeing things far away?**

____

Getting Ready to Read

SAY AND KNOW	Draw a line under the right answers or fill in the blank.
model	**1. Something using electricity** is ______________________.
computers	**2. A machine for writing** is a **computer typewriter calculator.**
electronic	
solve	**3.** Two machines that do arithmetic are **calculators classrooms computers.**
develop	
calculator	**4.** It means **a certain style or kind. model work magic**
typewriter	**5.** Scientists often work in **machines laboratories minutes.**
handy	
laboratories	**6. Something that is useful** is ______________________.

F-7 Modern Helpers

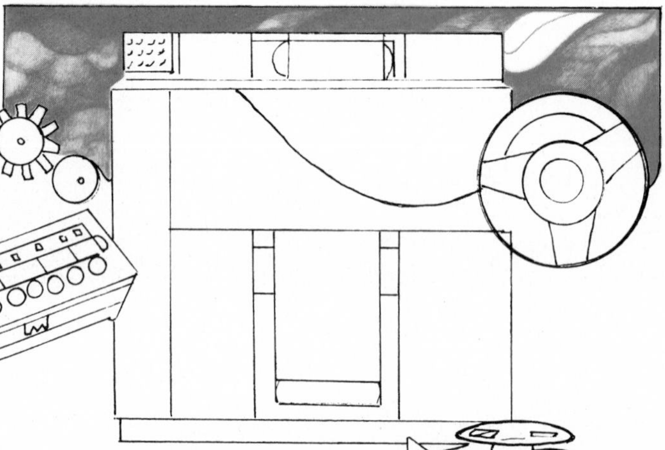

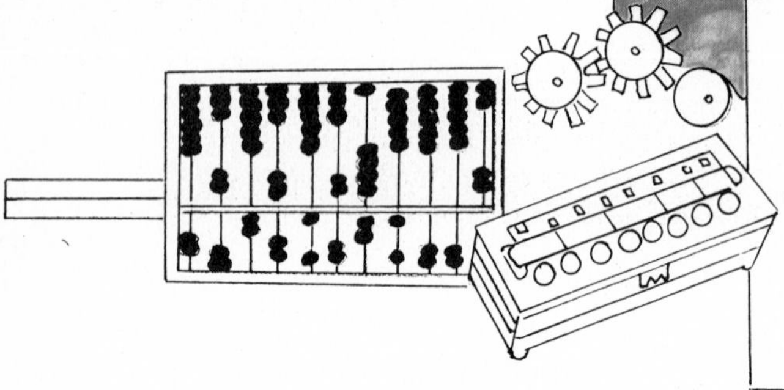

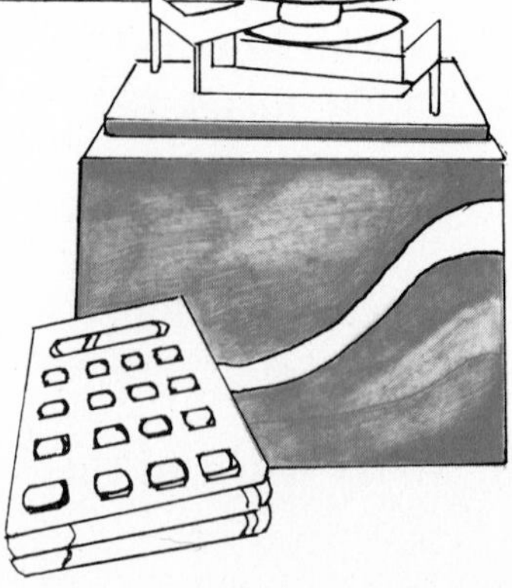

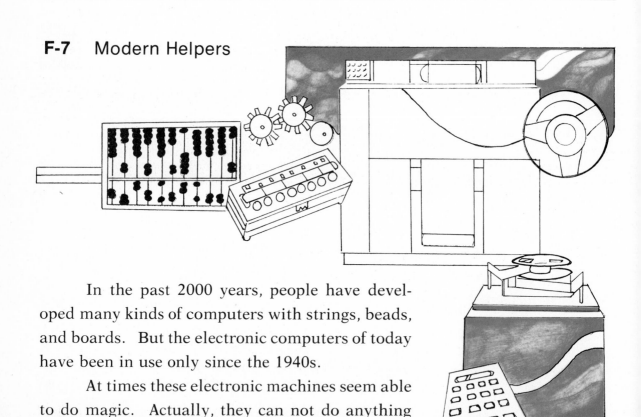

In the past 2000 years, people have developed many kinds of computers with strings, beads, and boards. But the electronic computers of today have been in use only since the 1940s.

At times these electronic machines seem able to do magic. Actually, they can not do anything that people can not do. Computers help because they work much faster than people do. Scientists

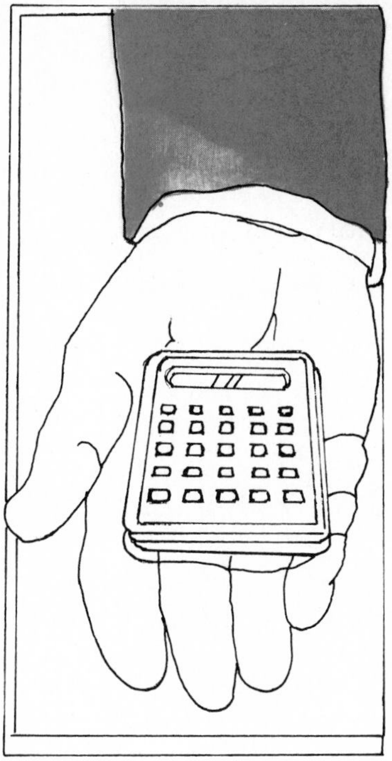

depend on computers every day to help in their work. Without computers, solving some problems might take months instead of minutes!

Early computers were about as big as typewriters. Today, problems can be solved on a huge machine or on a pocket calculator. Most of the small calculators are only a little larger than your hand. In the beginning, any computer cost thousands of dollars. Now many small models cost less than 50 dollars. Some cost as little as 10 dollars.

Once computers were found only in laboratories. Now these small mechanical helpers are found in many homes and classrooms. They are used to do everyday arithmetic.

F-7 Testing Yourself

NUMBER RIGHT

Draw a line under the right answer or fill in the blank.

1. Computers sometimes seem able to do ________________.

2. From the story, you can tell that

a. scientists of today need computers very little.
b. all pocket calculators cost a great deal.
c. the work of scientists includes hard problems.

3. The story as a whole is about

a. using computers.
b. ancient computers.
c. learning to add.
d. buying machines.

4. Calculators can add and subtract. Yes No Does not say

5. New models may cost as little as ten dollars. Yes No Does not say

6. What word in the last sentence means **daily?** ________________

Getting Ready to Read

SAY AND KNOW

rabbi

Torah

Talmud

Hebrew

strict

especially

village

Draw a line under the right answer or fill in the blank.

1. It means **a teacher of Jewish law.** **Torah** **Talmud** **rabbi**
2. It is **the scroll containing the Hebrew holy writing.** **Torah** **rabbi** **strict**
3. A rule that must be followed very carefully is **especially** **strict** **village.**
4. It means about the same as **particularly.** **strict** **rabbi** **especially**
5. **The writings of Jewish law or tradition** are in **the** **Talmud** **village** **rabbi.**
6. **The ancient language of the Jews** is ______________________.

F-8 First One, Then Many

Ernestine Rose lived in Poland over 100 years ago. Her father was a rabbi in their small village. At that time, only Jewish boys studied the holy books—the Torah and the Talmud. Ernestine's father knew how important these ancient Hebrew writings were. So he taught her to read them, too.

During that time, young people, especially girls, had to obey strict rules. They married when

their parents said they should. They married the person whom their parents chose. Ernestine would not accept that idea for herself. It was not long before she left her village to make a life of her own.

This was an unusual move, especially for a young Jewish woman. Most of the Jews at that time stayed very close to their villages. They stayed even though their lives were often in danger.

Finally, in the 1890s, other Jews began to leave Europe and Russia. Like Ernestine Rose, they began looking for new homes. Many came to America to start a new life where they would be safe.

F-8 Testing Yourself

NUMBER RIGHT

Draw a line under the right answer or fill in the blank.

1. Ernestine Rose lived in ______________________.

2. From the story, you can tell that
- a. long ago, young Jewish women didn't travel much.
- b. all young Jewish women left for England.
- c. traveling has always cost a lot of money.

3. This story as a whole is about
- a. writing Hebrew.
- b. roses in Poland.
- c. Jews who left the old villages.
- d. Jews getting married.

4. Ernestine left with her sister. Yes No Does not say

5. Ernestine missed her family very much. Yes No Does not say

6. What word in the third paragraph, first sentence, means **in particular?**

____

Getting Ready to Read

SAY AND KNOW	Draw a line under the right answer or fill in the blank.
prevent	1. It means **the opposite of wild.** **controlled** **alarm** **prevent**
controlled	2. **To keep from happening** is **to** **discover** **prevent** **alarm.**
discover	3. **To find** means **to** **discover** **contact** **control.**
operator	4. **The warning** is the same as **the** **operator** **alarm** **department.**
contacting	5. **Getting in touch with** is **contacting** **discovering** **alarming.**
department	6. **A person whose job is giving information over the phone** is **an**
alarm	____________________.

F-9 Fire! Fire! What to Do

To prevent fires, every city has its fire-fighters, firehouses, engines, and trucks. A fire can be controlled or stopped easily if it is discovered in time. Suppose you were the first to see a fire starting. How would you get word to the firehouse quickly?

One way would be to telephone. You would tell the operator where the fire is. The operator would telephone the firehouse.

A quicker way of contacting the fire department would be to use a fire alarm box. Such boxes are always painted red. If you live in a city, do you know just where to find the one nearest your home? It is easy to use a fire alarm box. When help is

needed, first open the box. Inside you will see a handle. Pull the handle down, and let go. Then stay at the box until the firefighters come.

F-9 Testing Yourself

NUMBER RIGHT

Draw a line under the right answer or fill in the blank.

1. A fire alarm box is always painted ____________.

2. From the story, you can tell that
  a. telephone operators are prepared to help in case of fire.
  b. it is best to try to put a fire out by yourself.
  c. fires in this country are not dangerous.

3. This story as a whole is about
  a. why cities have firefighters.
  b. telephones and fire alarm boxes.
  c. letting firefighters know about a fire.
  d. the work of firefighters.

4. Fires result in the loss of many lives. Yes No Does not say

5. Every city tries to prevent and control fires. Yes No Does not say

6. What word in the third paragraph, sixth sentence, means **within?**

____

The Farmers' Helper

The wheat was ripe and had to be harvested as quickly as possible. Mr. and Mrs. Hill and their helpers would have to work long hours in the field. Annie Hill would send them a lunch.

"Mary," she said on the first day, "the lunch is ready."

Mary, a girl of ten, took the lunch pail and started down the lane. Scout, the family dog, went, too. It was a long walk, and the morning was warm. "How would you like to carry the pail, Scout?" said Mary.

Scout had never carried a dinner pail, but the dog took the handle in its mouth.

They went on past the orchard, the big oak tree, and a patch of beets. Finally, they got to the wheat field. In those days, binding machines were used to cut the long stalks of wheat. The binders would tie wheat into bundles, and push the bundles down to the ground. Mr. Hill drove the binder. The helpers set the bundles of wheat into shocks, or stacks.

"Here is your lunch," called Mary. Scout set the pail on the ground in front of Mr. Hill.

"So, you got Scout to carry it for you," he said. "That's not a bad idea." Mr. Hill gave Scout a sandwich.

One day, Mary could not go to the field. "You must take the lunch alone today, Scout," said Annie Hill as she handed the pail to the dog. Scout took the handle in its mouth and started down the lane. The dog went past the orchard and the big oak and came to the beet patch. Just then, the dog heard a grunting sound. One of Mr. Brown's pigs was rooting up the beets! Scout barked and chased the pig away. As soon as Scout returned to the lunch pail, however, the pig was back. The chase might have lasted all day had not Mrs. Brown happened along. Finally, she and Scout drove the pig far away from the beets.

Scout was hot and tired. The poor dog wanted to rest. Instead, it picked up the dinner pail and walked slowly the rest of the way to the field.

Farmer Hill had just said, "I wonder if they have forgotten to send our lunch today?"

"Here it comes now," one helper called, seeing Scout.

"So, you brought the lunch all by yourself," said Mr. Hill as Scout set down the pail. "Here are two sandwiches for you."

Until they saw Mrs. Brown next day, they did not know why Scout had been late with their lunch.

MY READING TIME ______ (410 WORDS)

Thinking It Over

1. How do you know that Scout was a well-trained dog?
2. Explain how wheat is harvested today.
3. Before they spoke to Mrs. Brown, how might the farmers have explained Scout's lateness?

Getting Ready to Read

SAY AND KNOW

satellite
communicate
invent
electricity
cable
radar
astronauts
orbit

Draw a line under the right answer or fill in the blank.

1. **To make something new** means **to** **cable** **invent** **radar.**
2. **To speak or write** is **to** **radar** **communicate** **satellite.**
3. It is **something moving around in space.** **satellite** **cable** **radar**
4. It means **a heavy rope of wire.** **an orbit** **a cable** **electricity**
5. **A path in space around Earth** is **a radar** **an orbit** **a cable.**
6. **Someone who travels into space** is **an** ____________.

G-1 Talking Through Space

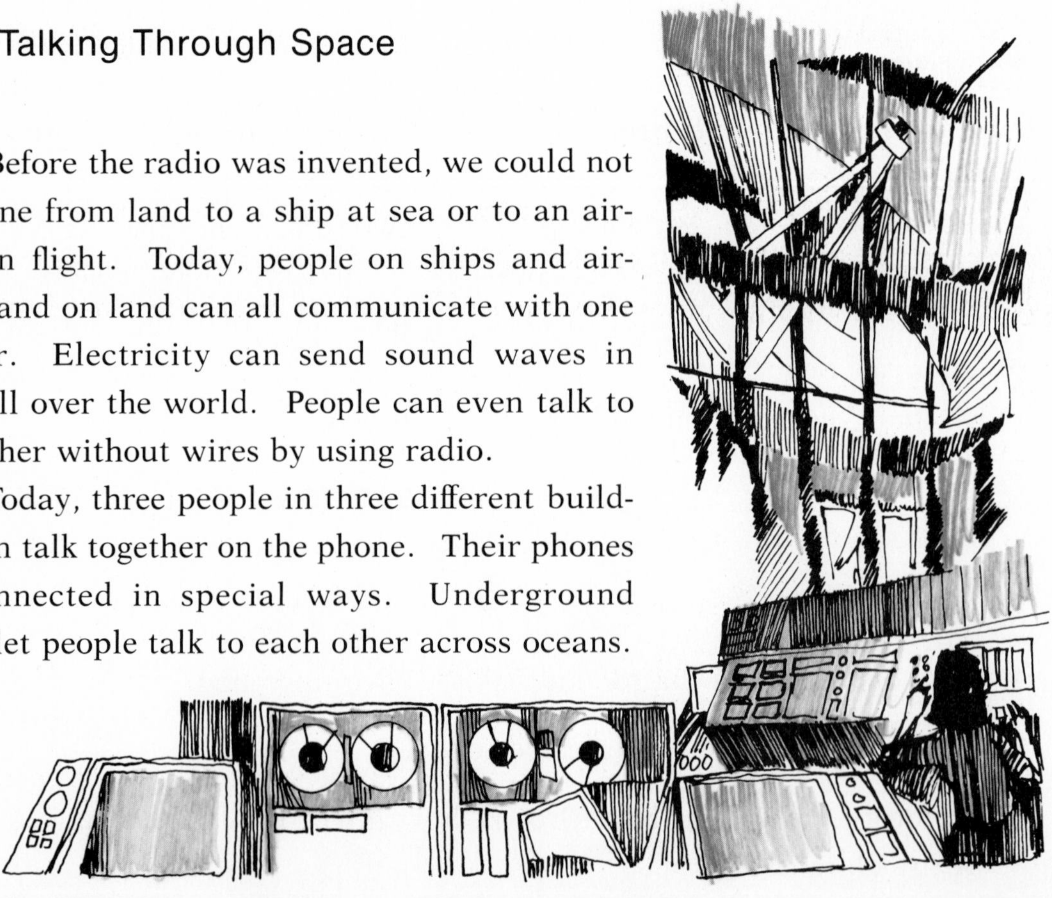

Before the radio was invented, we could not telephone from land to a ship at sea or to an airplane in flight. Today, people on ships and airplanes and on land can all communicate with one another. Electricity can send sound waves in wires all over the world. People can even talk to each other without wires by using radio.

Today, three people in three different buildings can talk together on the phone. Their phones are connected in special ways. Underground cables let people talk to each other across oceans.

Radio, television, and radar send their messages many miles through the air. Radar sends out waves. These waves bounce back from anything, even from the clouds. We use radar to track storms and to help with weather reports.

Satellites in orbit help us communicate, too. TV waves bounce off the satellites. Then the TV picture can be seen in many countries. When the astronauts landed on the moon, people all over the world were able to watch.

G-1 Testing Yourself

NUMBER RIGHT

Draw a line under the right answer or fill in the blank.

1. Electricity sends sound waves in ______________.

2. From the story, you can tell that
   - a. it is easier to communicate with other countries now.
   - b. we can communicate only by telephone now.
   - c. telephones are no longer used across the ocean.

3. This story as a whole is about
   - a. the days before the radio.
   - b. the days before the telephone.
   - c. talking by telephone.
   - d. ways to communicate.

4. It is possible to telephone by radio. Yes No Does not say

5. It is possible to radio from an airplane in the air to a ship at sea.
   Yes No Does not say

6. What word in the third paragraph, first sentence, means **what people communicate?** ______________

Getting Ready to Read

SAY AND KNOW

training
special
warned
tease
raid
strength
taught
fake

Draw a line under the right answer or fill in the blank.

1. If you are **practicing,** you are **training teasing warned.**
2. **A kind of attack** is a **fake warning raid.**
3. **Something unusual** is **special training taught.**
4. If you are told not to do something, you are **practiced teased warned.**
5. It means **make fun of. tease raid fake**
6. It is **the opposite of weakness.** ____________________

G-2 An Early Start

Hunting was an important way to get food and clothing for Native American tribes. Usually, the men would hunt animals with traps. Then the women would drag the kill home.

The boys and girls started their training with special games. Sometimes, the tribes would have fake raids on other tribes. At other times, they practiced hunting and swimming. A kind of football game was played, with the goal posts almost 1.6 kilometers (a mile) apart!

Since the women often built the homes, girls had to keep strong. They had ways to test their strength. Sometimes, a girl was given a bunch of wood to carry. Slowly, she was given more and more of a load. Finally, each girl would be so strong that she could carry enough wood for a whole night in one trip.

Girls in some tribes were taught to make fine wigwams. The women of the tribe warned them not to fail. If they did, they would have to live outdoors. They were told that they would be teased by the others.

G-2 Testing Yourself

NUMBER RIGHT

Draw a line under the right answer or fill in the blanks.

1. Hunting was an important way to get ________ and ________.

2. From the story, you can tell that
   a. Native Americans played games only for fun.
   b. Native Americans had their own ways of keeping in shape.
   c. football and baseball were the favorite games.

3. This story as a whole is about
   a. safety rules for football.
   b. how to build houses.
   c. the early training of some Native Americans.
   d. the rules of some Native American tribes.

4. Native American children liked their games. Yes No Does not say

5. Native Americans never hunted for food. Yes No Does not say

6. What word in the second sentence means **for the most part?**

____

Getting Ready to Read

SAY AND KNOW

flax

linen

bother

calves

vegetables

source

smokehouse

plentiful

preserve

Draw a line under the right answer or fill in the blank.

1. It means **the place from which something comes.** **bother** **source** **flax**
2. **Young cows and bulls** are **flax** **calves** **linen.**
3. If there is a lot of something, it is **alert** **plentiful** **linen.**
4. It means **trouble.** **smokehouse** **bother** **preserve**
5. **To keep something from spoiling** is **to** **source** **preserve** **bother.**
6. **Cloth made from flax** is __________.

G-3 Doing It All at Home

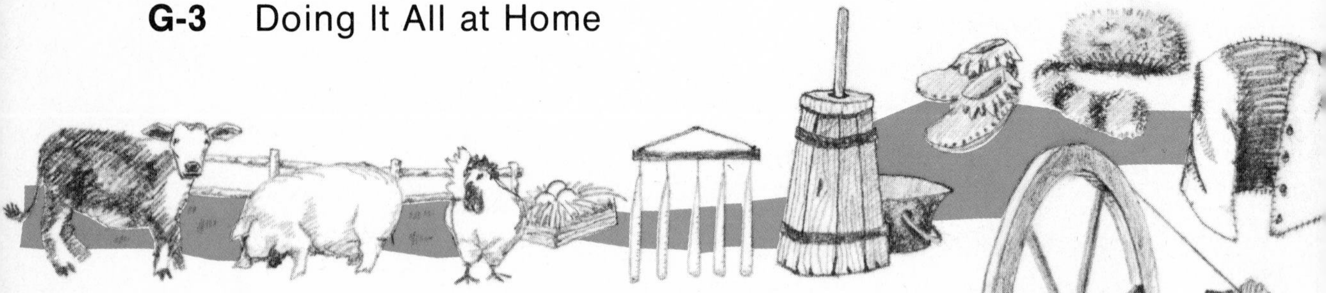

Most pioneer families used what was at hand. They got few things from far away. Often, their clothing was homemade. Sometimes, deerskins and furs from other animals were used to make clothes. Some pioneers raised flax for making linen cloth. In their homes, pioneers wove

cloth from wool, cotton, or linen yarn. They had spun the yarn on spinning wheels.

When food was plentiful, some was set aside for winter. To preserve meat, the pioneers dried it, salted it, or smoked it in smokehouses. Summer vegetables had to be kept from freezing and thawing during the year. They were put into cellars or into deep holes in the ground. Then the pioneers covered the vegetables with straw and earth.

Pioneers were sometimes bothered by wild animals. Foxes, wolves, and other animals found the pioneers' farms a good source of such food as chickens, pigs, sheep, and calves. The pioneers had to be ready for anything.

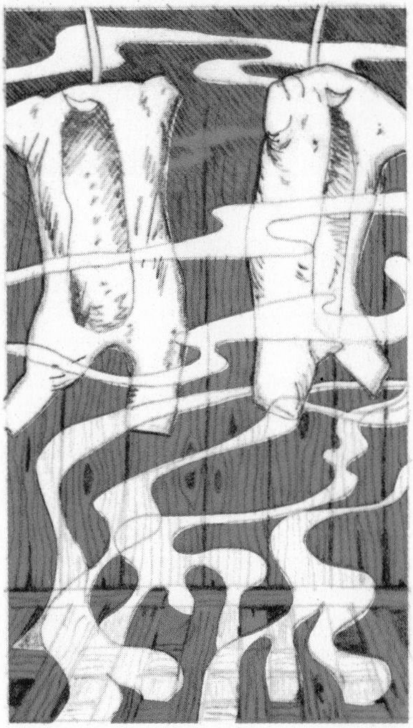

G-3 Testing Yourself

NUMBER RIGHT

Draw a line under the right answer or fill in the blanks.

1. Pioneers were sometimes bothered by ______________________________.

2. From the story, you can tell that
   a. pioneers could do many different things.
   b. pioneers liked making their own things better than buying them.
   c. pioneers made the things they needed in factories.

3. This story as a whole is about
   a. storing food for winter.
   b. making thread.
   c. a rough-and-ready life.
   d. fighting wild animals.

4. Yarn may be either wool or cotton. Yes No Does not say

5. All pioneers made their own furniture. Yes No Does not say

6. What word in the second paragraph, second sentence, means **keep from spoiling?** ______________________

Getting Ready to Read

SAY AND KNOW

hives
duties
drone
workers
special
thousand
pollen
necessary
guard

Draw a line under the right answer or fill in the blank.

1. **Something needed** is **workers** **duties** **necessary.**
2. It means **protect.** **drones** **guard** **hive**
3. It is **a yellow dust.** **duties** **hive** **pollen**
4. **Jobs** are **hives** **workers** **duties.**
5. **Of a certain kind** means **special** **necessary** **hatch.**
6. **Ten hundreds** is **one** ______________________.

G-4 The Honeybee Family

A honeybee family is large and interesting. Thousands of bees live together in one house, called a *hive.*

Each bee family has one queen bee. She is larger than the other bees. As the mother of the hive, she has special duties. The queen lays hundreds of eggs. In the spring, large numbers of baby bees hatch.

Each bee family also has drones. They are the father bees. Drones are strange fathers. They do no work. After the babies are hatched, it is necessary to save food. So, the drones are killed.

The workers make up the biggest part of the hive's family. They guard the queen. They care for the babies. They gather food for the whole family from the pollen of flowers. They also make the comb in which honey is stored for winter.

G-4 Testing Yourself

NUMBER RIGHT

Draw a line under the right answer or fill in the blank.

1. The largest bee in the hive is the ____________________.

2. From the story, you can tell that
   - a. each bee family has a queen bee and a king bee.
   - b. baby bees eat the same food that grown-up bees eat.
   - c. drones and workers are the same.

3. This story as a whole is about
   - a. baby bees.
   - b. a big, interesting family.
   - c. where honey comes from.
   - d. drones being killed.

4. Every bee in the hive must work. Yes No Does not say

5. Bees gather honey and store it for winter. Yes No Does not say

6. What word in the second sentence means **with one another?**

____

Getting Ready to Read

SAY AND KNOW	Draw a line under the right answer or fill in the blanks.
cling	**1. To look for** means **to search hook equip.**
clinging	**2. To stick close** is **to cling barb introduce.**
barb	**3. A point sticking out from another point** is **a barb hitchhiker cling.**
hook	
search	**4.** Things that are **the same** are **alike barbed cling.**
alike	**5. People who catch rides with strangers** are **hitchhikers seeds alike.**
sticktights	
hitchhikers	**6.** Write the two words in **sticktights.** ________ ________.

G-5 Nature's Hitchhikers

There are different kinds of sticktights, but they are all shaped very much alike. They all have hornlike parts. There are many fine barbs, or tiny hooks, on the sticktights. Some sticktights have

only two horns. Others have three or four. A few have as many as six.

The seeds of all the sticktights are great hitchhikers. Sticktight seeds ride on people or animals. These seeds have horns with barbs on the ends. So the sticktights are ready to go traveling in search of new homes. With these barbed horns, the seeds can stick tight. They ride a long way. Did you ever have seeds steal a ride on you by clinging to your clothes?

Besides sticktights, there are many other travelers among the plant seeds. Try to find some others. Show them to your class.

G-5 Testing Yourself

NUMBER RIGHT

Draw a line under the right answer or fill in the blank.

1. Each sticktight seed has horns with __________ on the end.

2. From the story, you can tell that
- a. sticktight seeds usually travel on the wind.
- b. sticktights travel by springing onto the ground.
- c. sticktights can travel only by sticking to something that moves.

3. This story as a whole is about
- a. different kinds of sticktights.
- b. sticktights as travelers.
- c. all plants with barbed horns.
- d. people who travel.

4. All sticktights have the same number of horns. Yes No Does not say

5. Every sticktight seed gets a ride. Yes No Does not say

6. What word in the third sentence means about the same as **hooks?**

____

Getting Ready to Read

SAY AND KNOW	
	Draw a line under the right answer or fill in the blank.
stroke	**1.** It means **a gift for doing something.** **talent** **mystery** **artist**
mystery	**2.** It is **the name of a black community.** **Lawrence** **Harlem** **Alston**
popular	
Harlem	**3.** It is **the opposite of not liked.** **artist** **popular** **stroke**
handwriting	
talent	**4. Something hard to figure out** is a **mystery** **popular** **stroke.**
artists	**5.** It means **marks** or **lines.** **strokes** **talent** **artists**
Lawrence	
Alston	**6.** Which word is made up of two smaller words? ________

G-6 One of the Greats

Jacob Lawrence had his first art show in the 1930s. By the 1940s, he was becoming one of the great painters of our time. Many artists at that time were painting to tell a story. They painted about war. They painted about people without jobs. But Lawrence was an artist first. He did not paint just to tell a story.

Sometimes, he painted black leaders, like Frederick Douglass or Harriet Tubman. Sometimes, he just painted the world around him.

Even as a child, Lawrence loved art. He spent many hours in Harlem watching people and painting. His mother knew he had great talent. Although she was not rich, she did everything she could to help him. Finally, he began to study with the great black artist Charles Alston.

Lawrence never liked to paint just to be popular. His paintings had a kind of mystery. His strong colors and vigorous brush strokes made people pay attention to them. He once said: "Painting is like handwriting. Everyone has their own way." His way was strong and fine.

G-6 Testing Yourself

NUMBER RIGHT

Draw a line under the right answer or fill in the blank.

1. Lawrence painted with strong ____________________.

2. From the story, you can tell that
   a. Lawrence really wanted to be a writer.
   b. Lawrence believed people should paint simple stories.
   c. Lawrence believed artists should follow their own ideas.

3. The story as a whole is about
   a. great leaders of the 1930s.
   b. a great mystery.
   c. telling stories.
   d. a great artist.

4. Lawrence studied with a great artist. Yes No Does not say

5. Lawrence's mother was also a painter. Yes No Does not say

6. What word in the fourth paragraph, first sentence, means **well-liked?**

____

Getting Ready to Read

SAY AND KNOW

mechanical

computer

invert

calculator

bored

mathematician

punching

Draw a line under the right answer or fill in the blank.

1. **To be tired of doing something** is **to be**
   bored happy helped.
2. **Someone who is an expert at math** is
   a machine an astronaut a mathematician.
3. **Something having machine parts** is
   a mathematician simple mechanical.
4. **To make a new thing** is **to invent help start.**
5. **Something that computes** is **a computer gallon number.**
6. **A machine that does arithmetic** is **a** ____________________.

G-7 A Daily Helper

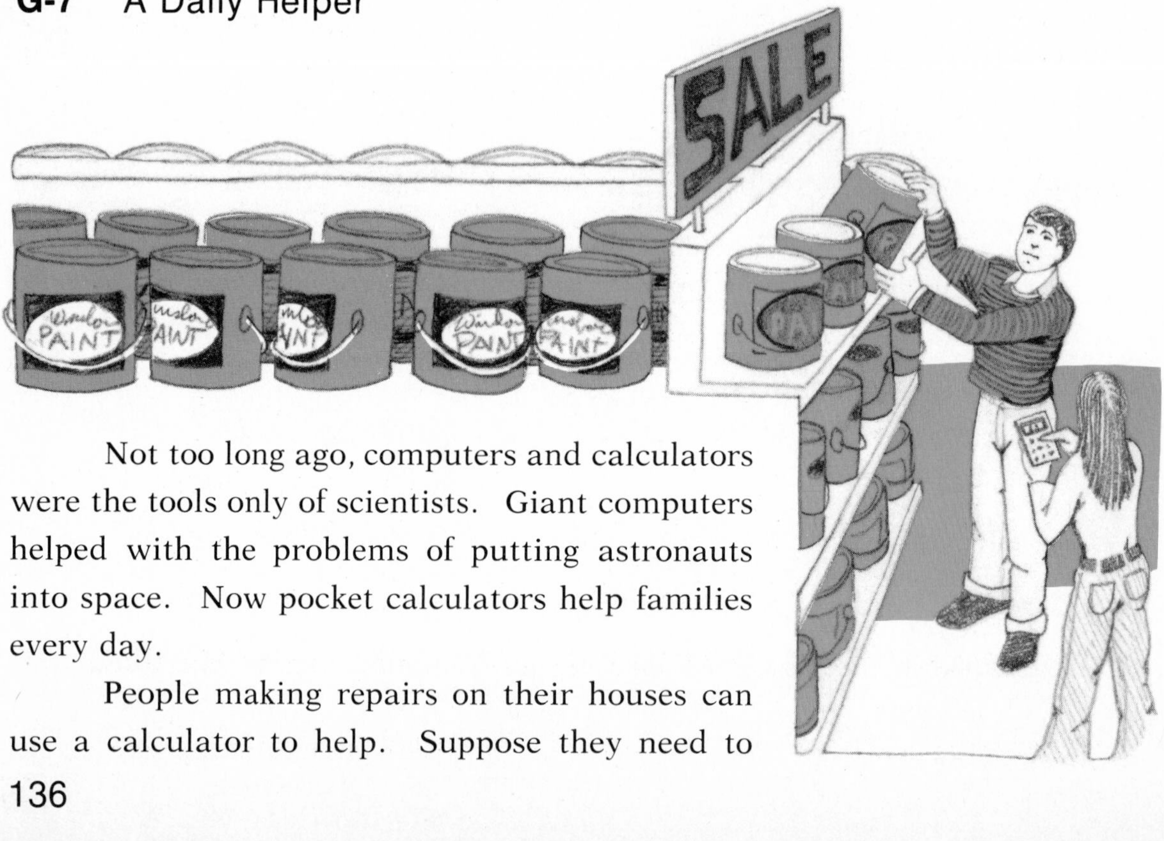

Not too long ago, computers and calculators were the tools only of scientists. Giant computers helped with the problems of putting astronauts into space. Now pocket calculators help families every day.

People making repairs on their houses can use a calculator to help. Suppose they need to decide how much paint to buy. They may find they need 31.2 liters (8¼ gallons) of paint. The store is selling paint at $1.25 per liter (about ¼ gallon). By punching the buttons of a calculator, they can quickly tell how much 31.2 liters (8¼ gallons) will cost.

One of the first mechanical adding machines was invented in 1642 by Blaise Pascal. He was a famous mathematician. It seems that he got tired of adding long rows of numbers. To keep from being bored, he invented a simple calculator. Pascal's idea is still used in calculators today. We need this help now just as much as he did then!

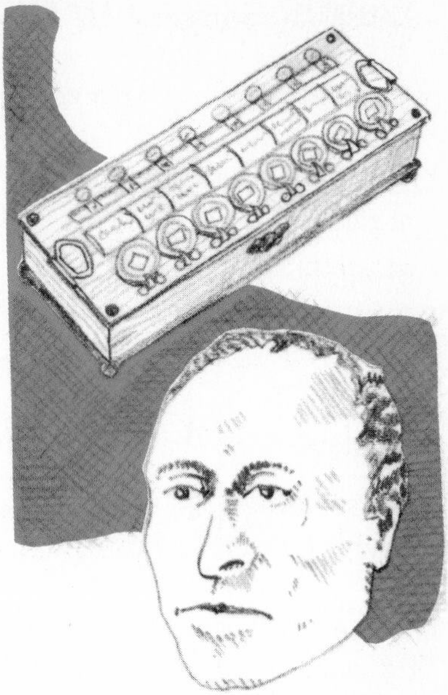

G-7 Testing Yourself

NUMBER RIGHT

Draw a line under the right answer or fill in the blank.

1. Giant computers helped put astronauts into ____________.

2. From the story, you can tell that
- a. using calculators makes math much easier.
- b. calculators help only scientists.
- c. the early calculators worked best.

3. This story as a whole is about
- a. the first calculator.
- b. how to add.
- c. uses for calculators.
- d. buying paint.

4. Pascal invented an adding machine. Yes No Does not say

5. Adding machines are no longer used. Yes No Does not say

6. What word in the second sentence means **huge?** ____________

Getting Ready to Read

SAY AND KNOW

travel
architect
develop
collectors
tapestry
practice
workshop
Harrania
Egypt
Egyptian

Draw a line under the right answer or fill in the blank.

1. **Someone who plans buildings** is **a collector** **an architect** **a workshop.**
2. **To change and grow** means **to** **develop** **travel** **practice.**
3. **A weaving for a wall** is **an architect** **a workshop** **a tapestry.**
4. **To do again and again** is **to** **collect** **practice** **travel.**
5. **Someone who collects** is **an architect** **a collector** **an Egyptian.**
6. It means **a place to do work.** ____________________

G-8 Young Weavers

For some Egyptian children, life today is not very different from the way it was hundreds of years ago. These children never leave their desert homes. Life goes on as it has for years. Much time is spent making yarn and cloth. Parents teach children how to spin and to weave.

In 1952, an Egyptian architect, Ramses Wissa Wassef, set up a way for this work to develop. He started a workshop in Harrania, Egypt. There, children would have a chance to practice weaving tapestries. The children knew very little about the world outside. They followed their own thoughts about the way their work should look.

Over time, museums found out about the children's tapestries. By the 1970s, the children of

the Harrania workshop were known by great collectors throughout the world.

People from this part of Egypt hardly ever leave to live in other parts of the world. Their works of art travel, instead. In this way, others across the ocean can still learn about them and their way of life.

G-8 Testing Yourself

NUMBER RIGHT ______

Draw a line under the right answer or fill in the blanks.

1. The children of the workshop never leave their desert __________.

2. From the story, you can tell that
   a. the children's work was very fine.
   b. the children did not like to travel.
   c. the Harrania workshops failed.

3. This story as a whole is about
   a. American workshops.
   b. how museums collect art.
   c. children of Harrania.
   d. life in Egypt.

4. The children of Harrania still live there. Yes No Does not say

5. People from Egypt love to travel. Yes No Does not say

6. What words in the last paragraph, first sentence, mean **almost never?**

__________ __________

Getting Ready to Read

SAY AND KNOW	Draw a line under the right answer or fill in the blank.
Mexico	**1.** It is **a kind of plant.** **burn** **red** **aloe**
blister	**2. A painful swelling that comes from a burn** is a **blister** **spot** **plant.**
macaroni	**3.** It means **directions for cooking.** **instant** **recipe** **special**
aloe	**4. Screamed** means **shrieked** **blistered** **coughed.**
recipe	**5.** It is **a kind of noodle.** **plant** **edge** **macaroni**
shrieked	**6.** A country south of the United States is ________________.

G-9 A Medicine Plant

Maria and Paul were making their favorite dinner, macaroni and cheese. The pot of water was beginning to boil on the stove. Maria's eyes were on the recipe. She reached for the salt.

"Ow!" she shrieked. Her hand had hit the edge of the pot. She started to run for the first-aid cream. "Wait!" Paul shouted. "Use this instead." He reached for a plant on the window sill. He quickly tore off a little piece. He squeezed the juice onto Maria's burned finger.

In a few seconds, the pain stopped. There was no blister. There was only a little red spot. The "magic" plant was an aloe. Paul remembered what his grandmother had told him about this instant cure for burns. Grandmother had told him about other plants from Mexico, too. There were plants to use for sores and bites and coughs and fevers. Growing certain plants could be like having a special medicine chest!

G-9 Testing Yourself

NUMBER RIGHT

Draw a line under the right answer or fill in the blank.

1. The pot was hot because it was beginning to __________.

2. From the story, you can tell that
   a. Paul helped Maria by thinking fast.
   b. Paul asked Maria what the best medicine was.
   c. Paul didn't really want to help Maria.

3. This story as a whole is about
   a. growing plants.
   b. preventing burns.
   c. plants that help to cure.
   d. learning to cook.

4. A rose plant helped Maria. Yes No Does not say

5. Paul used magic to help Maria. Yes No Does not say

6. What word in the first sentence means **best-liked?** __________

The Mirror of Matsuyama

Long ago, in the town of Matsuyama in Japan, there lived a man, a woman, and their little daughter. They loved each other very much and were happy together. Once the man made a long journey. He went to the far-off city of Tokyo. When he returned, he brought fine gifts to his wife and daughter.

The last gift he gave to the woman was in a small, white box. She opened it and took out something round and bright. It looked like a pool of clear water. When she looked into it, she saw a fine, strong face.

"It is a mirror," explained the man. "You see yourself in it. All the people in Tokyo have mirrors." At first the woman looked often at herself in the mirror. After a while, however, she put it away. "How foolish it is for me to gaze at myself in a mirror," she said to herself.

"How much better for me to remember only that my face can be happy and smiling. It shows how I feel. If I am calm and happy, others will know that. If I am sad or angry, they will know that too. Those who care for me are sad when I am sad." With these words, she put the mirror away. After that, she looked into it twice each year, just to see if her face still looked strong and happy.

The years passed. The man and woman grew older. Their little girl grew up to be strong and loving, too. One day, the mother grew very ill. She knew that she must die. Calling her daughter to her, she showed the mirror to the girl. The young girl looked into it for the first time.

"Mother dear," she cried, "I see you here! You do not look thin and pale as you are now. You look strong and smiling as you always have."

"When I am gone," the mother said, "look into this each morning and each night. If anything troubles you, tell me about it. Always try to do right, so you will see only strength and happiness here."

Twice daily the girl looked at the bright, happy face she remembered as her mother's. She told it all that had happened. When the day had been a happy one, the face smiled back at her. She was careful not to do anything unkind, for she knew how sad the face would look when she told of it.

The girl grew more strong and kind. She grew more like the mother whose face she saw each day and loved.

MY READING TIME ______ (410 WORDS)

Thinking It Over

1. How did the mother know what the mirror showed?

2. What did the daughter think the mirror showed?

3. Why didn't the mother tell her daughter whose face was really reflected in the mirror?

Getting Ready to Read

SAY AND KNOW

- flaming
- mercury
- wick
- kerosene
- developed
- neon
- fluorescent
- candle
- common
- melted

Draw a line under the right answer or fill in the blank.

1. It is **a kind of gas.** **wick** **fluorescent** **neon**
2. **Changed from solid to liquid** means **melted** **flaming** **common.**
3. **A wax stick burned to give light** is **a** **wick** **neon** **candle.**
4. If something **grew,** it **melted** **developed** **flamed.**
5. **The opposite of unusual** is **candle** **common** **flame.**
6. **An oil for burning** is ____________________.

H-1 The Story of Light

Long ago, people had only the sun and moon for light. After they learned to make fire, they carried flaming sticks to light their way. Later, they learned to dip the sticks into melted fat before lighting them. The burning fat gave a brighter light and lasted longer. After people learned to use a twist of fiber as a wick, they made candles.

Candles were improved as time went by and are still used today.

Then came grease lamps and olive-oil lamps. After these, there were kerosene lamps. They burned coal oil and had glass chimneys. Later, the gaslight, which needed neither wick nor chimney, was developed.

All these lights had one thing in common. They had to be lighted with a flame.

Finally, electric lights were invented. These are not lighted with a flame. There are electric lights that use neon and fluorescent gases. Some street lights now use a gas called *mercury vapor*.

H-1 Testing Yourself

NUMBER RIGHT

Draw a line under the right answer or fill in the blank.

1. The first light that people made using a wick was the ________________.

2. From the story, you can tell that
   a. gaslights were invented before candles.
   b. candles are needed less today than they once were.
   c. today's candles are made of neon gases.

3. This story as a whole is about
   a. better and better lights.
   b. lights of long ago.
   c. electric lights.
   d. making candles.

4. All lights must be lighted with a flame. Yes No Does not say

5. Gaslights use wicks. Yes No Does not say

6. What word in the first paragraph, third sentence, means **to put in and lift out again?** __________

Getting Ready to Read

SAY AND KNOW

least
nevertheless
slightest
shuck
meal
follow
pumpkins
squashes
frighten

Draw a line under the right answer or fill in the blank.

1. **To scare** is **to** **frighten** **least** **shell.**
2. **To go after** means **to** **follow** **shell** **meal.**
3. **To take the shell off** means **to** **shuck** **meal** **squash.**
4. It means **even so.** **least** **nevertheless** **slightest**
5. It means **a kind of fine grain.** **squashes** **meal** **pumpkins**
6. It is **the opposite of most.** ____________________

H-2 Learning by Doing

Native American children of long ago did not go to school as children do today. Nevertheless, they had many things to learn. They had to learn to walk in the woods without making the least noise. Any sound might frighten the deer that was being hunted. Sometimes, when hunting, the children had to lie for an hour making no noise at all.

Young Native Americans learned to make a fire by rubbing sticks together. They learned to tell what kind of weather was coming. Boys learned to follow the tracks of wild animals. The children knew the ways, hiding places, and calls of animals and birds.

In the spring, the girls helped the women plant. They grew fine crops of corn, beans,

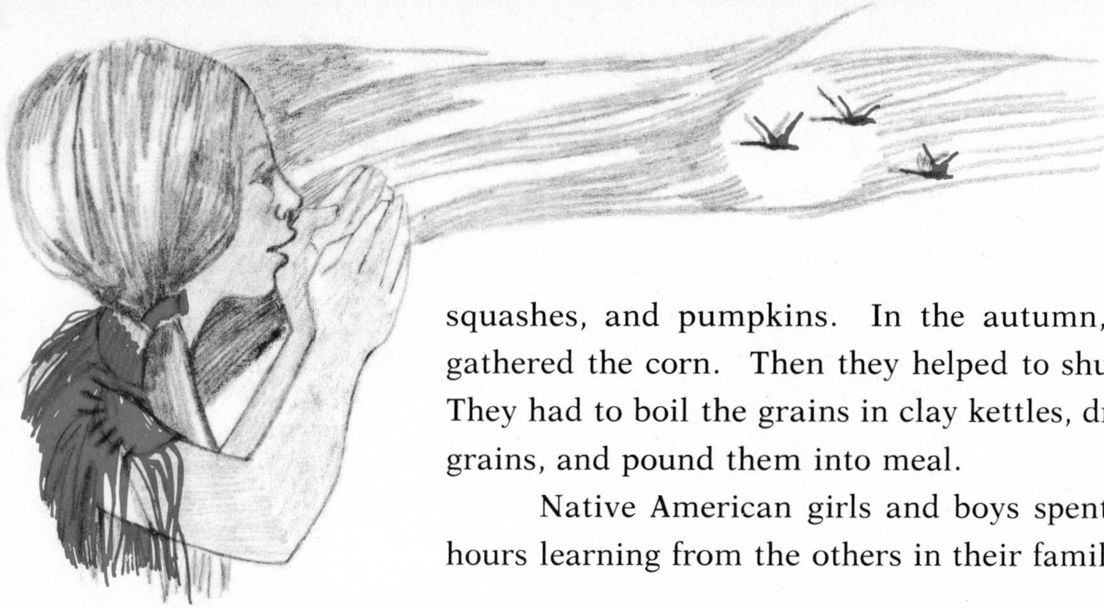

squashes, and pumpkins. In the autumn, they gathered the corn. Then they helped to shuck it. They had to boil the grains in clay kettles, dry the grains, and pound them into meal.

Native American girls and boys spent long hours learning from the others in their families.

H-2 Testing Yourself

NUMBER RIGHT ______

Draw a line under the right answer or fill in the blank.

1. Native American children did not go to ______________________.

2. From the story, you can tell that
   a. Native American children went to school to learn to read.
   b. Native American children learned those things they would need to use later on.
   c. Native American children played games all the time.

3. This story as a whole is about
   a. schools of long ago.
   b. being quiet for an hour.
   c. what the Native American children had to learn.
   d. what the Native American children liked.

4. The Native American boy had much time to play.
Yes No Does not say

5. The Native American girl went to school. Yes No Does not say

6. What word in the third sentence means **sound?** ______________________

Getting Ready to Read

SAY AND KNOW	
tender timber spoil hardships jerky tasty waste Oregon California	Draw a line under the right answer or fill in the blank. 1. It means **wood or trees in a forest.** **timber** **tender** **jerky** 2. **To throw away a good thing** is **to** **jerky** **timber** **waste.** 3. It means about the same as **decay** or **rot.** **jerky** **tasty** **spoil** 4. **A kind of dried meat** is **jerky** **timber** **obey.** 5. It means **not tough.** **jerky** **tender** **timber** 6. What word means **difficulties?** ____________________

H-3 Moving West

The longest trips west were made by pioneers who traveled to the Oregon country and to California. From what they had heard, the pioneers thought the weather in the West seemed perfect. There was plenty of water and timber. The soil was rich, and there was beautiful pasture land.

Often, families traveled in a long train of covered wagons. Before starting out, the people chose a leader whom everyone agreed to obey. Trips to the West often took many months. The pioneers faced many hardships. They had to cross rivers, mountains, and deserts.

Along the way, there were plenty of buffalo for food. At first, the pioneers took the parts they liked best. They left the rest for the wolves. The Cheyenne used the hides and meat and fat. They left only the bones. Later, the pioneers also learned how to leave no waste.

The families also learned to fix beef jerky. The buffalo meat was cut into strings and dried completely. It was not tender, but it was tasty and it did not spoil on the long trip.

H-3 Testing Yourself

NUMBER RIGHT

Draw a line under the right answer or fill in the blank.

1. The weather in the West seemed ____________________.

2. From the story, you can tell that
  a. the pioneers made careful plans before they started.
  b. the pioneers were afraid to cross rivers.
  c. the pioneers liked to kill buffalo.

3. This story as a whole is about
  a. traveling by raft to Oregon.
  b. hunting on the plains.
  c. pioneers choosing their trip leader.
  d. making the cross-country trip west.

4. Some pioneers loved to hunt. Yes No Does not say

5. Pioneers took cows and horses with them. Yes No Does not say

6. What word in the last sentence means **go bad?** ____________________

Getting Ready to Read

SAY AND KNOW	
odd	Draw a line under the right answer or fill in the blank.
underground	**1.** It is **a kind of animal.** **mole** **bore** **odd**
mole	**2. Beneath the land** means **earthworm** **underground** **tunnel.**
earthworm	**3. Something strange** is **hardly** **odd** **bores.**
hardly	**4.** It means about the same as **digs.** **bores** **moles** **forefeet**
forefeet	**5. Scarcely** or **barely** means **hardly** **tunnel** **oddly.**
bores	
tunnel	**6. Front feet** are called ____________________.

H-4 Hunting Underground

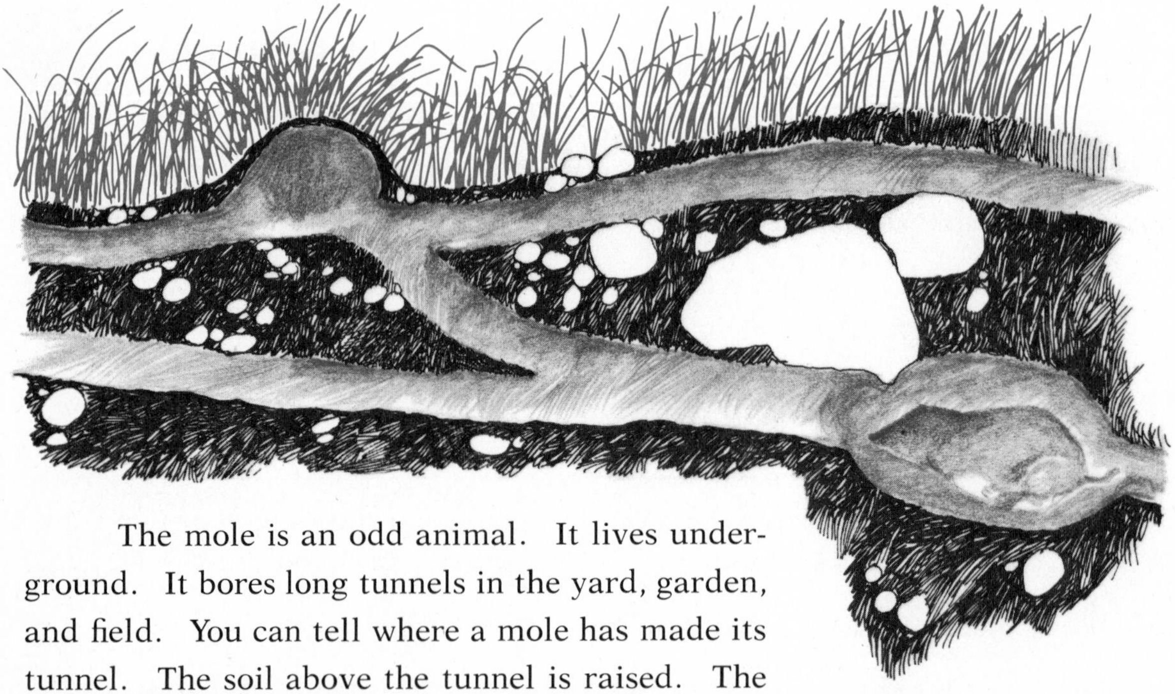

The mole is an odd animal. It lives underground. It bores long tunnels in the yard, garden, and field. You can tell where a mole has made its tunnel. The soil above the tunnel is raised. The mole spends its life digging. It makes its home in the dark, and it tunnels for food.

Moles do some harm in the garden. They also help by eating harmful insects. In addition, moles eat earthworms and mice.

The mole is a strange-looking little animal. It has no neck and has very tiny eyes and ears. It can hardly see or hear. In your hand, it is a flat ball of mouse-colored fur, about 15 centimeters (6 inches) long. Its pink tail is about 2½ centimeters (1 inch) long. With its spadelike forefeet and its nose, it can dig better than any other animal. In one night of hunting, it may dig many long underground tunnels.

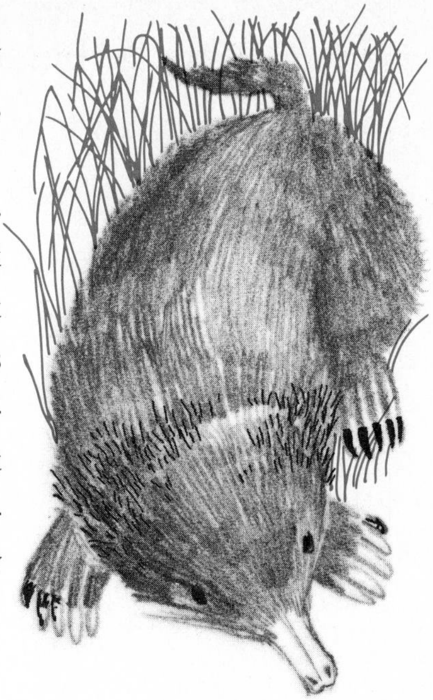

H-4 Testing Yourself

NUMBER RIGHT ______

Draw a line under the right answer or fill in the blank.

1. The mole's forefeet are shaped like ______________________.

2. From the story, you can tell that
   a. moles are safest underground.
   b. moles can climb trees.
   c. moles and mice are just alike.

3. This story as a whole is about
   a. the farmer's main enemy.
   b. an underground digger.
   c. feet shaped like mice.
   d. digging for a living.

4. The mole's tail is about 6 meters long. Yes No Does not say

5. The mole does only harm in a garden. Yes No Does not say

6. What word in the second paragraph, second sentence, means **bugs?**

____

Getting Ready to Read

SAY AND KNOW

nearly
bulb
tulip
sprouts
lily
Holland
Dutch
daffodil
berry
crocus

Draw a line under the right answers or fill in the blank.

1. **One flower from Holland** is **the** **onion** **tulip** **berry.**
2. People who live in Holland are **nearly** **Dutch** **lilies.**
3. Which two are flowers? **daffodil** **vine** **crocus**
4. It means **begins to grow.** **plants** **bulbs** **sprouts**
5. **A juicy fruit with many seeds** is **a** **berry** **lily** **tulip.**
6. It means **almost.** ____________________

H-5 New Life

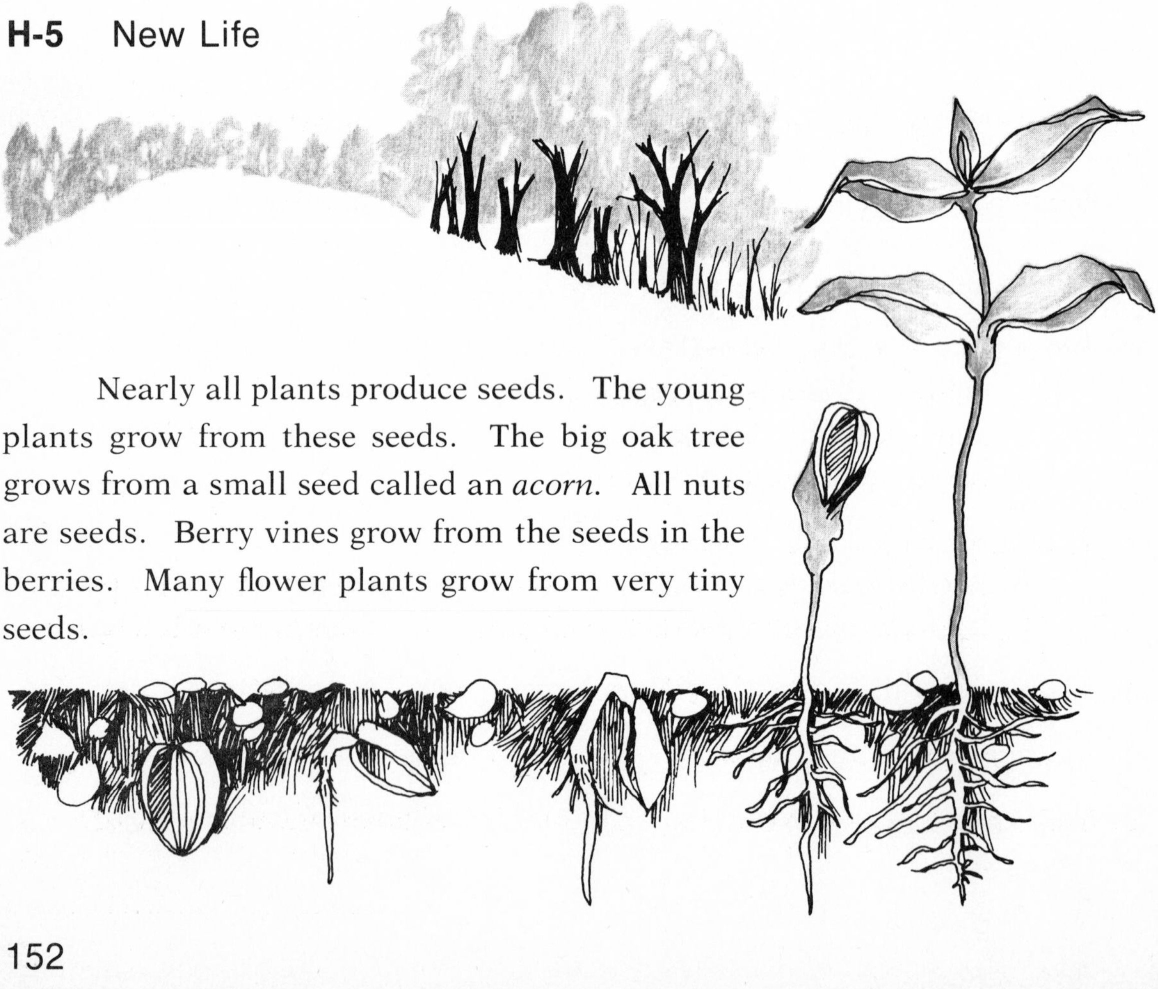

Nearly all plants produce seeds. The young plants grow from these seeds. The big oak tree grows from a small seed called an *acorn*. All nuts are seeds. Berry vines grow from the seeds in the berries. Many flower plants grow from very tiny seeds.

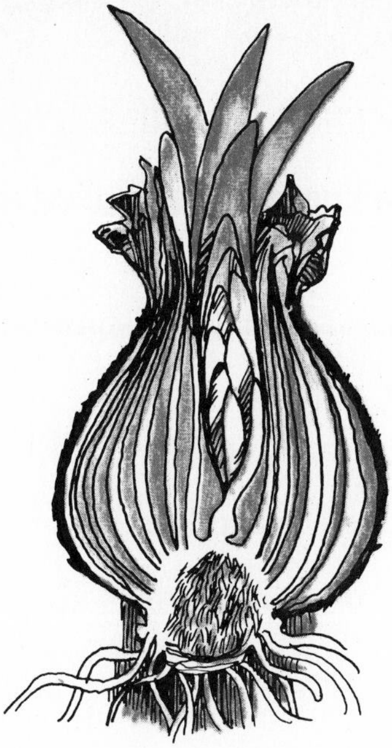

Some plants grow seeds and form bulbs. Young plants grow from the bulbs. You may have seen a picture showing how a small bulb sprouts from the side of the parent bulb. You may have planted bulbs in the fall. Did you see early flowers in the spring? The Dutch in Holland raise great numbers of tulip bulbs to sell. Daffodils and crocuses grow from bulbs, too.

The lily, also, is grown from a bulb. The onion belongs to the lily family. For early onions, the bulbs are planted in the very beginning of spring. In the South, onion seeds are planted for the larger onions to be harvested in the fall.

H-5 Testing Yourself

NUMBER RIGHT

Draw a line under the right answer or fill in the blanks.

1. For early onions, you plant the ______________________.

2. From the story, you can tell that
   a. tulips grow only in Holland.
   b. some seeds are good to eat.
   c. onions and lilies look alike.

3. This story as a whole is about
   a. different kinds of seeds and nuts.
   b. growing plants from seeds and bulbs.
   c. which plants grow bulbs.
   d. the lily and the onion.

4. All plants grow bulbs as well as seeds. Yes No Does not say

5. All plants growing bulbs also grow seeds. Yes No Does not say

6. What words in the last paragraph, second sentence, mean **is part of?**

______________ ______________

Getting Ready to Read

SAY AND KNOW

products
shampoos
special
especially
mansion
charity
millionaire
invent
formula

Draw a line under the right answer or fill in the blank.

1. **A special soap for hair** is **invent** **a shampoo** **a product.**
2. **Something made or produced** is a **product** **charity** **shampoo.**
3. It means **someone who has millions of dollars.** **mansion** **millionaire** **charity**
4. **Money given away** is **charity** **special** **product.**
5. It means **a large, fancy house.** **millionaire** **mansion** **special**
6. It means **mainly.** ____________________

H-6 Making Money

As a young woman, Sarah Breedlove Walker took in laundry for a living. Later in her life, she was the first black woman in the United States to become a millionaire. She made her fortune with a secret formula. It was a kind of hair care just for blacks. Walker developed creams and soaps and a shampoo made with coconut oil.

She built her business in a way no black woman had done before. She went door to door carrying her products. The families she met were delighted with her items for hair care. Soon business was booming. She opened a school to train salespeople. Before long, 2000 people were selling her products.

In her grand mansion, Walker's life was very different from her early life. She had treasures such as gold-plated pianos. But she never forgot people in need. She gave her money freely to charity. She opened a school for girls in West Africa. Even as a millionaire, she never lost her kindness.

H-6 Testing Yourself

NUMBER RIGHT

Draw a line under the right answer or fill in the blank.

1. Sarah Breedlove Walker opened a school for girls in ____________________.

2. From the story, you can tell that

a. Walker became rich through hard work and good ideas.
b. Walker became rich because she was lucky.
c. Walker's first goal was to open schools to train people.

3. The story as a whole is about

a. the first black woman millionaire.
b. rich salespeople in soaps and cosmetics.
c. a gold mansion.
d. charity clubs.

4. Walker sold her soaps door to door. Yes No Does not say.

5. Walker lived alone in her mansion. Yes No Does not say

6. What word in sentence three means about the same as **recipe?**

____

Getting Ready to Read

SAY AND KNOW

computer

calculator

realize

borrow

amount

earn

information

bank

Draw a line under the right answers or fill in the blank.

1. **To find out** is to **borrow earn realize.**
2. **To get something by promising to return it** means **to computer borrow amount.**
3. It means **to make money by working. borrow amount earn**
4. Which two are machines that do arithmetic? **calculator information computer**
5. It means **how much there is. amount realize earn**
6. **A place that keeps money** is **a** __________.

H-7 For Large and Small Businesses

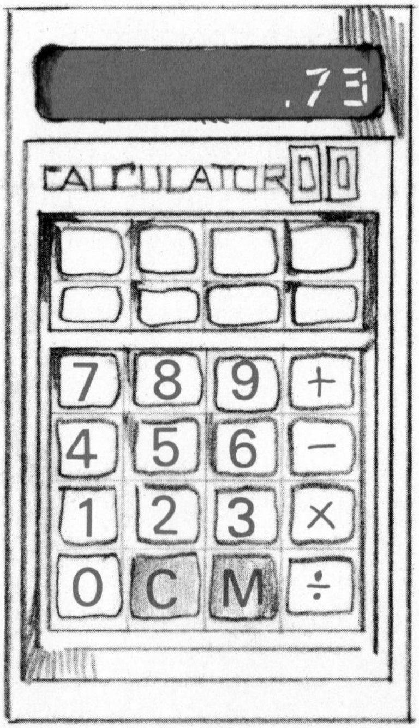

Sue's mother had a small business. Her car was an important part of her work. Now it was time for a new one. She sat down with her pocket calculator. Sue was surprised. "What does that have to do with buying a new car?" she asked. Then her mother began to explain.

First she had to figure all of her costs for each month. That would show her if she had enough money left for a new car. She knew she could trade in her old car. So she would subtract that amount from the cost of a new one. That would tell her how much she needed to borrow from the bank. She could then use the calculator to tell how much she would have to pay back to the bank each month. Sue had never realized how important arithmetic was in everyday living.

The work of large business and government offices would be very slow without computers or calculators. All the information about the money that Americans earn is kept on computers. Someone figured out how much computer tape the earnings information took. It was 640 kilometers (more than 400 miles) of tape!

H-7 Testing Yourself

NUMBER RIGHT

Draw a line under the right answer or fill in the blank.

1. Sue's mother had a small ______________________.

2. From the story, you can tell that
   a. only large companies have uses for computers and calculators.
   b. Sue's mother wanted to own a big business.
   c. arithmetic is important to all business people.

3. This story as a whole is about
   a. how to borrow money.
   b. the importance of arithmetic.
   c. adding without calculators.
   d. small businesses.

4. Large offices use computers. Yes No Does not say

5. Sue's mother needed a car for business. Yes No Does not say

6. What word in the next-to-last sentence means **worked out?**

____

Getting Ready to Read

SAY AND KNOW

famine
famous
unsinkable
survive
lifeboat
actually
struck
spirit
Irish
Ireland
Molly Brown
Titanic

Draw a line under the right answer or fill in the blank.

1. It means **continue to live.** **survive** **empty** **strike**
2. **A time of great hunger** is a **spirit** **famine** **famous.**
3. If it won't sink, it is **aboard** **unsinkable** **great.**
4. It means **in fact.** **high** **actually** **jokes**
5. It means about the same as **mood.** **spirit** **saved** **still**
6. What word means **a boat to rescue people?**

____

H-8 They Came from Ireland, Too

Many Irish people who came to the United States in the 1800s came from a sad background. They had been poor and hungry for many years. When the potato famine struck, it was a time of greater sadness. Thousands died. Those who could raise enough money for the trip came to America.

The Irish loved their old country. Many actually put a bit of Irish soil in a bag. When their ship landed in the United States, they emptied the

bag. Then, in their new land, they were still stepping on the soil of Ireland.

The Irish had a strong spirit. They loved to joke and tease. One woman from an Irish family became famous because of her spirit. Molly Brown was a passenger on the great ship *Titanic* when it sank. She was one of the ones who survived. In her lifeboat, she kept spirits high with her songs and jokes.

Molly Brown kept rowing until she was saved. A famous play was written about her. It was called *The Unsinkable Molly Brown.*

H-8 Testing Yourself

NUMBER RIGHT

Draw a line under the right answer or fill in the blank.

1. Many Irish immigrants to America in the 1800s had a sad

____________________.

2. From the story, you can tell that

a. the Irish like to be sad.
b. the Irish usually like to sing.
c. the Irish do not like to give up.

3. This story as a whole is about

a. growing potatoes.
b. Irish women who joke.
c. the Irish who came to America.
d. saving lives in shipwrecks.

4. The Irish became farmers here. Yes No Does not say

5. The Irish ate only potatoes. Yes No Does not say

6. What word in the last sentence means **not able to sink?**

____

Getting Ready to Read

SAY AND KNOW	Draw a line under the right answer or fill in the blanks.
outer	**1.** If it breaks easily, it is **outer** **delicate** **beyond.**
delicate	**2. A tool** means about the same as **an** **eardrum** **instrument** **opening.**
eardrum	
beyond	**3. On the outside** means **delicate** **outer** **passage.**
nerve	**4. A way through** is **a** **throat** **passage** **outer.**
passage	**5.** It means **farther than.** **beyond** **outer** **middle**
instrument	**6.** What two words make up **eardrum?** ____________ ____________.

H-9 How We Hear

Our ears are really like fine instruments. They need to be guarded. The part of the ear that we see is the outer ear. It helps to catch sound. Sound passes through the opening to the middle ear.

At the beginning of the middle ear is the eardrum. Within the middle ear are little bones that help to carry sound. A passage leads from the middle ear to the back part of the nose and upper part of the throat. It is like a little tunnel or a water pipe, about as big as a big paper clip.

Beyond the middle ear is the inner ear. In the inner ear, there is a nerve that acts like an electric wire. It carries sound to the brain. All parts of the ear are very delicate. They can be easily damaged.

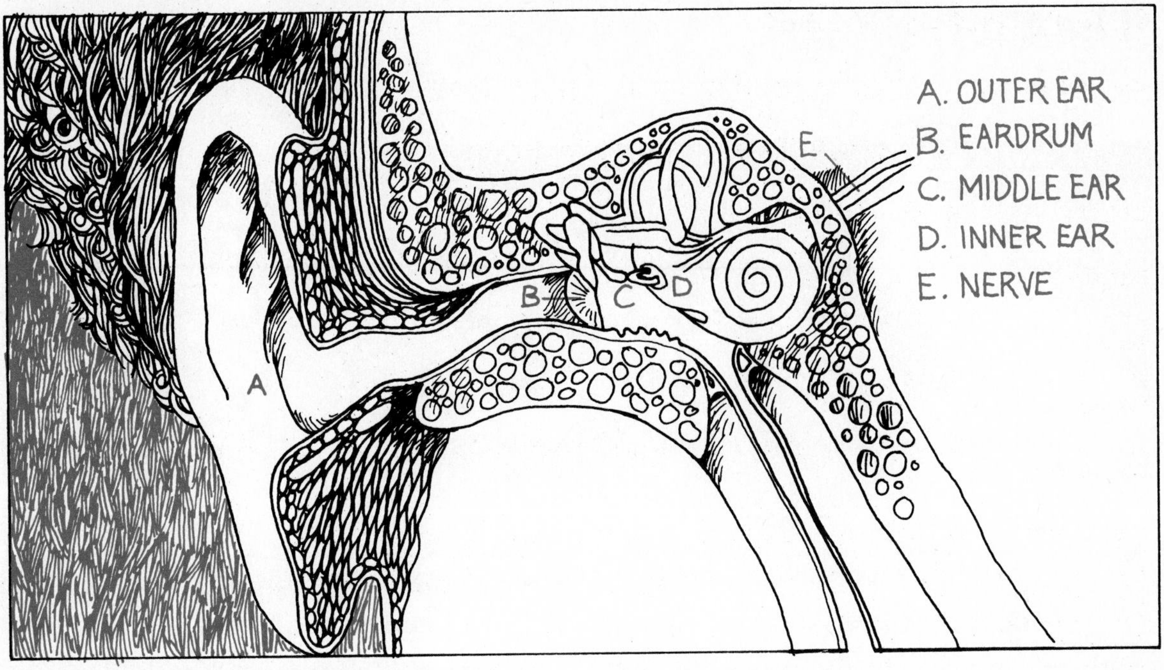

H-9 Testing Yourself

NUMBER RIGHT

Draw a line under the right answer or fill in the blank.

1. At the beginning of the middle ear is the ____________________.

2. From the story, you can tell that
   a. a person could probably hear even if the outer ear were hurt.
   b. we could hear better without the outer ear.
   c. germs cannot hurt the ear.

3. This story as a whole is about
   a. the different parts of the ear.
   b. taking care of our eyes.
   c. the dangerous passage.
   d. guarding the eardrum.

4. There really is an electric wire from the ear to the brain.
Yes No Does not say

5. We can see the outer ear. Yes No Does not say

6. What word in the second sentence means **protected?** ____________________

The Boiled Eggs

Once a traveler stopped overnight at an inn. In the morning, he ate a large breakfast of bread and boiled eggs. He found, however, that he had very little money with him. "I will return in a few days," he told the landlord. "Will you trust me until then?" The landlord said he would, and the traveler went on his way.

When the traveler had finished his business in town, he returned to the inn and asked for his bill. The landlord presented it to him. Imagine his surprise to find that it was four thousand dollars! At first he thought this was a joke. The landlord, however, explained.

"You ate ten eggs," he said. "If those had hatched, they would have been ten chickens. These may have laid eggs and hatched them. In four years, the amount would be four thousand dollars. Because I am kind, I won't figure beyond four years."

The traveler could not pay such a bill. He was told to appear before the chief judge to defend himself for not paying the debt. He told his story to a lawyer. She agreed to help.

On the day of the trial, the traveler and the landlord appeared in court on time. The lawyer did not arrive. They waited and waited. Finally, nearly an hour late, the lawyer came into the courtroom.

"Why were you not here on time?" the judge asked her sternly.

"I am very sorry," she said. "I was delayed in my cornfields."

"Cornfields!" cried the judge. "Why, the corn is not yet ripe."

"I know," said the lawyer. "This morning I boiled two bushels of corn. At noon I shall plant the corn. By next week it will be ripe, and I shall harvest it."

All the people in the courtroom laughed. The judge looked angry. The traveler wished he had not engaged this lawyer.

"How can you think that boiled corn will grow in your fields?" asked the landlord, who thought that the lawyer was crazy.

"How can you think that chickens will hatch from boiled eggs?" she said in reply.

Then the judge understood. "Were your eggs boiled?" he asked the traveler.

"They were," answered the man.

The judge fined the cunning landlord one hundred dollars. The traveler gave half of the money to the clever lawyer. Then he went home to tell his friends how he had been paid ten dollars for every boiled egg he had eaten.

—adapted from an old Danish folktale

MY READING TIME ________ (410 WORDS)

Thinking It Over

1. Why do you think the landlord figured the bill for only four years?
2. Could the lawyer have won the case as easily if she had arrived on time?
3. Should the landlord have been paid by the traveler for the lodging and the breakfast, even though he tried to get more than fair payment from the traveler?

Getting Ready to Read

SAY AND KNOW	Draw a line under the right answer or fill in the blank.
concerned	**1.** It means **from the sun.** **solar** **prehistoric** **coal**
wood-burning	**2. A block of baked clay** is **a** **coal** **furnace** **brick.**
brick	**3. Before written history** means **concerned** **solar** **prehistoric.**
furnace	**4. One mineral that burns** is **brick** **coal** **furnace.**
prehistoric	**5.** If you are **worried,** you are **concerned** **prehistoric** **brick.**
transported	**6.** One can make an especially hot fire in a ________________.
coal	
solar	

I-1 Keeping Warm

For thousands of years, humans have been concerned with finding better ways to heat houses. In prehistoric days, they made wood-burning fires on rocks or on the ground.

Then, people learned how to make fireplaces of stones. They learned to make chimneys for the fireplaces. When they found out how to make brick, they used bricks to make fireplaces.

After iron was discovered, people made iron stoves for heating. These stoves used wood and coal for fuel. They heated small rooms very well.

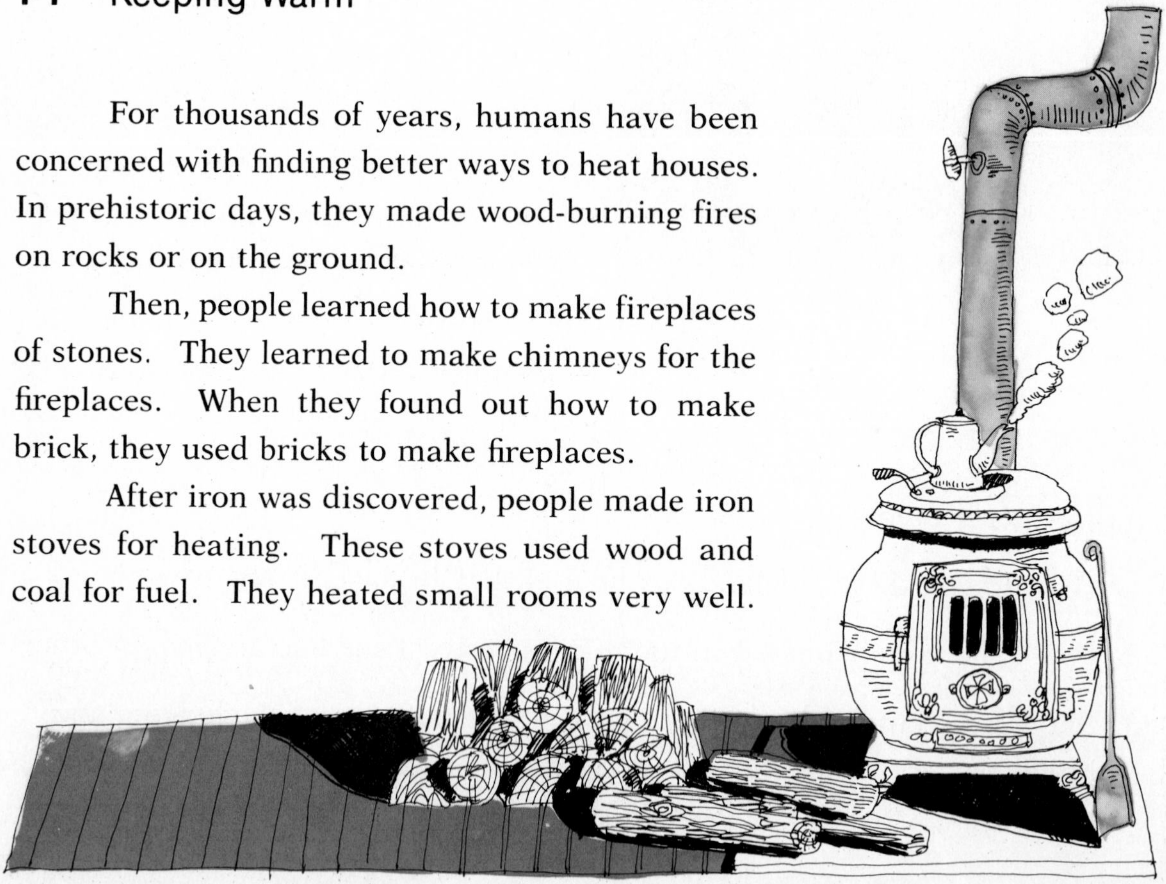

People in the country still like to use them. The small, round stoves are called *pot bellies.* Can you guess why?

Today, in many places, gas that comes from far under the ground can be transported from place to place in pipes. Many stoves today use gas for fuel. A furnace, which is like a big stove, sometimes uses gas. Sometimes oil is used. In addition, more and more homes are heated by electricity and solar energy.

I-1 Testing Yourself

NUMBER RIGHT

Draw a line under the right answer or fill in the blank.

1. A furnace is something like a big ______________________.

2. From the story, you can tell that
  a. heaters that burn gas are better than wood-burning heaters.
  b. people will work hard to keep from being cold.
  c. bricks make good fuel.

3. This story as a whole is about
  a. electric heaters.
  b. the fireplace.
  c. ways of heating houses.
  d. heating a tent house.

4. The best way of heating is with electricity. Yes No Does not say

5. Fireplaces are often made of brick. Yes No Does not say

6. What word in the first sentence means **improved?** ______________________

Getting Ready to Read

SAY AND KNOW	Draw a line under the right answer or fill in the blank.
supplies	**1.** Something that causes death is **deadly** **supplies** **pottery.**
pottery	**2. Patterns** are called **pottery** **diseases** **designs.**
deadly	**3.** It means the same as **illnesses.** **diseases** **improves** **designs**
designs	**4. The things people keep to fill their needs** are their
diseases	**designs** **supplies** **diseases.**
wove	**5. Dishes and pots made of clay** are **designs** **deadly** **pottery.**
improve	**6.** If they made it by weaving, they ________ it.

I-2 How Life Changed

By the 1750s, the Native Americans' way of life had been changed by Europeans. Some things that were brought to America, such as deadly diseases, were not good. Other changes helped improve life for the Native Americans.

Instead of using tools of stone and bone, the Native Americans started to use iron kettles and steel knives.

Before, they had used only dogs as work animals. Now they had horses. They learned to raise horses as well as chickens and sheep. From sheep's wool, some tribes wove beautiful rugs with special designs.

The Native Americans began to need their new neighbors. They wanted to trade furs to get better tools. Most of them stopped making their own pottery and tools. These arts were no longer passed on from parent to child. Soon the young workers had forgotten the old ways.

Many Native Americans did not want the settlers moving farther into their lands. But they had learned to want the settlers' supplies.

I-2 Testing Yourself

NUMBER RIGHT

Draw a line under the right answer or fill in the blanks.

1. The Native Americans' way of life was changed by ______________________.

2. From the story, you can tell that
   a. Native Americans learned to weave from the settlers.
   b. Native Americans did not like horses.
   c. most people want new things when they see them.

3. This story as a whole is about
   a. good changes in old lives.
   b. the early use of horses.
   c. settlers who helped Native Americans.
   d. Native Americans adopting new ways.

4. Today, Native Americans are sometimes farmers.
   Yes   No   Does not say

5. Europeans and Native Americans always fought.
   Yes   No   Does not say

6. What word in the first paragraph, third sentence, means **make better?**

____

Getting Ready to Read

SAY AND KNOW	Draw a line under the right answer or fill in the blank.
able	**1.** It means **different** or **across from.** **typical** **bench** **opposite**
bench	**2. A long seat** is called **a** **dipper** **able** **bench.**
halves	**3.** It means **two equal parts of a whole.** **shapes** **able** **halves**
opposite	**4. A cup with a long handle** is **a** **typical** **opposite** **dipper.**
dipper	**5. Of a usual type** means **able** **typical** **during.**
during	**6.** If something happens **within a certain time,** it happens
typical	______________________ that time.

I-3 Stand Up to Write

As soon as they were able, the pioneer farmers in a new country built log schoolhouses. Their children were sent to school during the winter months. Often the frontier school had only one room. The young children and the older ones shared the room. These pioneer schoolhouses were many different shapes and sizes.

Here is what you might have seen in a typical schoolhouse in the Oregon Territory. At one end was a big fireplace. It had a chimney built of sticks and mud. Across the room, opposite the fireplace, was the door. Just outside the door was a bench that held a bucket of water. Beside the bucket was a dipper from which all the children drank.

Benches made of logs split into halves ran along two sides of the room. The rough log walls formed the bench backs. On the other wall of the room was a long, wide shelf. When the children needed to write, they put their slates on the shelf and wrote standing up.

I-3 Testing Yourself

NUMBER RIGHT

Draw a line under the right answer or fill in the blank.

1. The pioneer schoolhouse was built of ____________________.

2. From the story, you can tell that
- a. pioneer teachers were very strict.
- b. pioneer children usually did not go to school.
- c. many pioneers thought schools were important.

3. This story as a whole is about
- a. country schoolhouses.
- b. the inside of a schoolhouse.
- c. the seats in a schoolhouse.
- d. the outside of a schoolhouse.

4. Pioneer teachers were all men. Yes No Does not say

5. In these schools, the big children taught the little children.
Yes No Does not say

6. What word in the fourth sentence means **used together?**

____

Getting Ready to Read

SAY AND KNOW	
gnaw	Draw a line under the right answer or fill in the blank.
forepaw	**1. To chew on** is to **gnaw supply dam.**
twig	**2. One who builds** is a **beaver builder dam.**
shallow	**3. A small branch** is a **dam twig gnaw.**
sturdy	**4.** It means **strong. sturdy forepaw dam**
supply	**5. Something stored** is a **build sturdy supply.**
builder	
beaver	**6.** What word means **the opposite of deep?** ________________

I-4 Teeth That Cut Wood

Beavers are fine builders. They live in water, which protects them from their enemies. Beavers work together to build a dam across a small river. The dam gives them a supply of water. They also help each other to build their houses.

To get the logs and branches they need, beavers cut down small trees. They do this by

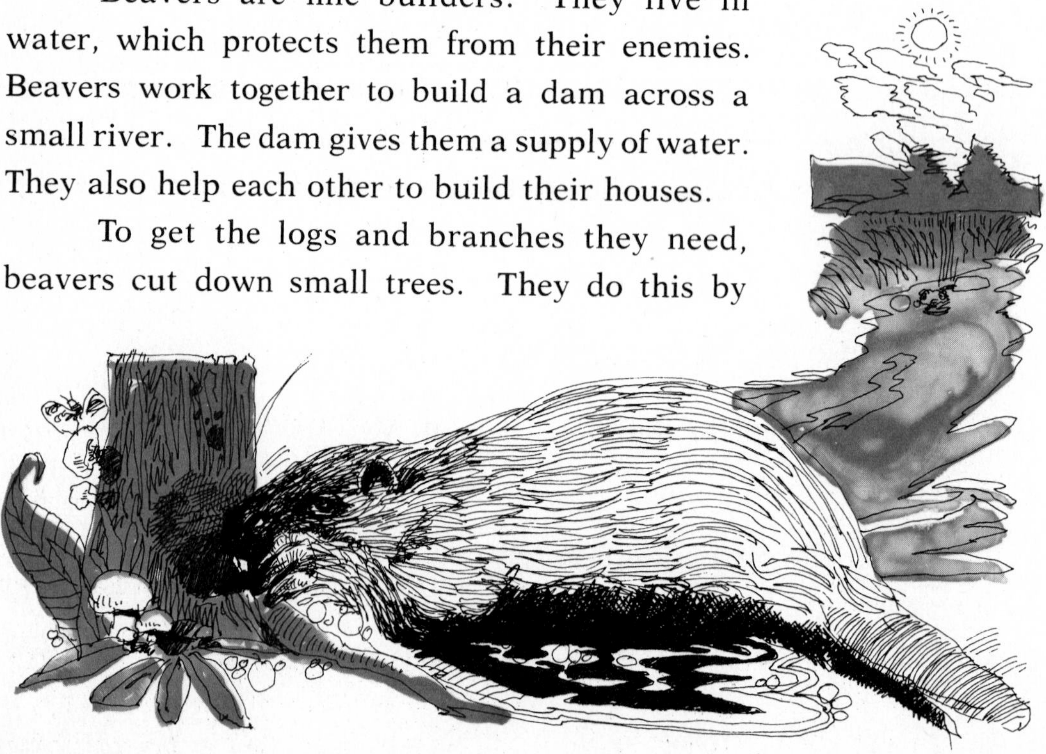

gnawing around the trunk with their sharp, strong front teeth. They chew off the branches. Then they gnaw the trunk into pieces. With their teeth, they drag the branches and the pieces of wood into the water. With their forepaws, they get stones and mud. They put up a sturdy dam of wood, stone, and mud.

In shallow water, the beavers build houses of sticks, grass, moss, and mud. Openings leading into these houses are at the bottom of the stream.

Beavers feed on twigs and bark. Before winter begins, they store twigs and sticks for food near the openings to their houses.

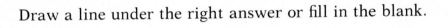

I-4 Testing Yourself

NUMBER RIGHT

Draw a line under the right answer or fill in the blank.

1. Beavers cut down trees with their ____________________.

2. From the story, you can tell that
   a. beavers can swim.
   b. beavers eat fish.
   c. beavers' fur is thick.

3. This story as a whole is about
   a. beavers as our helpers.
   b. the way beavers live.
   c. smart animals.
   d. lazy beavers.

4. Beavers are the best of the animal builders. Yes No Does not say

5. Every part of a beaver's house is under water. Yes No Does not say

6. What word in the third sentence means **a wall built to hold back water?**

____

Getting Ready to Read

SAY AND KNOW

bud
potato
tuber
tulip
stem
root
sunflower
artichoke
Jerusalem
underground

Draw a line under the right answer or fill in the blank.

1. It is **a vegetable.** **stem** **tuber** **potato**
2. It is **a fat underground stem.** **bud** **tuber** **tulip**
3. **The part of a plant that supports other parts** is **the** **artichoke** **stem** **sunflower.**
4. It is **a plant.** **bud** **root** **artichoke**
5. **A plant bump that will grow into a leaf or flower** is **a** **tuber** **root** **bud.**
6. It is **a city in Israel.** ____________________

I-5 Roots We Eat

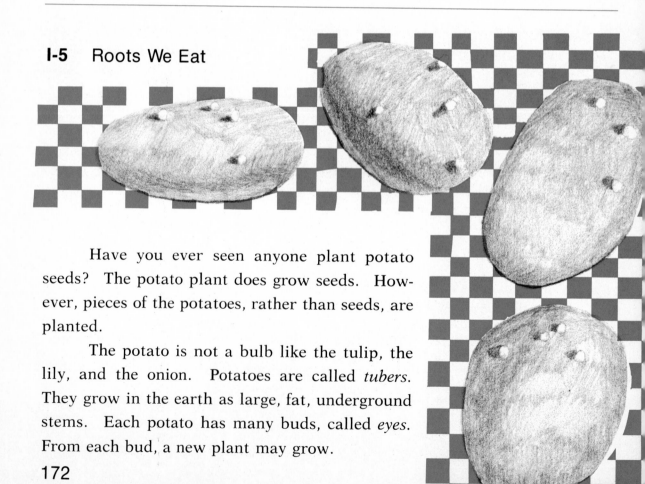

Have you ever seen anyone plant potato seeds? The potato plant does grow seeds. However, pieces of the potatoes, rather than seeds, are planted.

The potato is not a bulb like the tulip, the lily, and the onion. Potatoes are called *tubers.* They grow in the earth as large, fat, underground stems. Each potato has many buds, called *eyes.* From each bud, a new plant may grow.

We do not plant the whole potato. We cut it into pieces, with one or more eyes, or buds, to a piece. The piece of potato is food for the young plant until its roots can get a good start.

Another tuber is the Jerusalem artichoke. This plant looks something like a sunflower. Like the potato, it has a root, or tuber, which we can eat.

I-5 Testing Yourself

NUMBER RIGHT

Draw a line under the right answer or fill in the blank.

1. The potato is a ______________________.
2. From the story, you can tell that
   a. potato seeds are good to eat.
   b. artichokes are sunflowers.
   c. potato seeds are not usually used.
3. This story as a whole is about
   a. growing big potatoes.
   b. the potato's eyes.
   c. new plants from tubers.
   d. planting potato seed.
4. The potato is a vegetable. Yes No Does not say
5. The potato plant is the only one that grows tubers. Yes No Does not say
6. What word in the first sentence means **some person?** ______________

Getting Ready to Read

SAY AND KNOW

allow
birthplace
respect
governor
industry
projects
senator
election
solve
Luis Muñoz Marín
Puerto Rico
Spanish-American

Draw a line under the right answers or fill in the blank.

1. It means **businesses** or **factories.**
   industry **senator** **project**
2. It means **to find an answer for.** **election** **solve** **allow**
3. To treat someone well is to show
   industry **election** **respect.**
4. Which two are people in government?
   senator **project** **governor**
5. **A voting to choose someone** is
   a senator **an election** **a birthplace.**
6. It means **the city or country where you were born.**

   ____

I-6 The People's Choice

To the young Luis Muñoz Marín, two countries were home. His early life was spent in both his birthplace of Puerto Rico and in the United States. The United States took over the small island of Puerto Rico in 1898, after the Spanish-American War. There were great problems for the people. There was not enough work. Pay was low. Important people would not help the workers. Muñoz Marín knew he had to help.

As a writer, Muñoz Marín wrote newspaper articles about the island's problems. He found out that words were not enough. So he became a senator. He worked on projects to get the United States to put new industry in Puerto Rico. He wanted more jobs and better pay for people.

In 1947, Puerto Rico was allowed to hold its own elections. Whom would the people choose as governor? Muñoz Marín was the one they wanted. The workers loved him because they knew he respected them. And he had a deep love for his people. Muñoz Marín didn't solve all of the problems. But he brought great changes for the people of Puerto Rico.

I-6 Testing Yourself

NUMBER RIGHT

Draw a line under the right answer or fill in the blank.

1. The United States took over the small ____________________.

2. From the story, you can tell that
   a. Muñoz Marín was mainly interested in money.
   b. Muñoz Marín loved his homeland.
   c. Muñoz Marín had trouble finding work.

3. This story as a whole is about
   a. a Puerto Rican leader.
   b. becoming governor.
   c. writing for newspapers.
   d. the Spanish-American War.

4. Muñoz Marín had many children. Yes No Does not say

5. Muñoz Marín could not help his people. Yes No Does not say

6. What word in the second sentence means **the city or country where you were born?** ____________________

Getting Ready to Read

SAY AND KNOW

yardstick
calendar
ruler
span
decimals
system
measurement

Draw a line under the right answer or fill in the blank.

1. **A way of finding the exact size of something** is **measurement system yardstick.**
2. It is **a kind of ruler. calendar yardstick decimal**
3. It means **a certain way of doing things. ruler system span**
4. It is **a system based on ten. decimal yardstick span**
5. It means **a space of time. system yardstick span**
6. **A table showing the days, weeks, and months of the year** is a ____________________.

I-7 Important Systems of Measurement

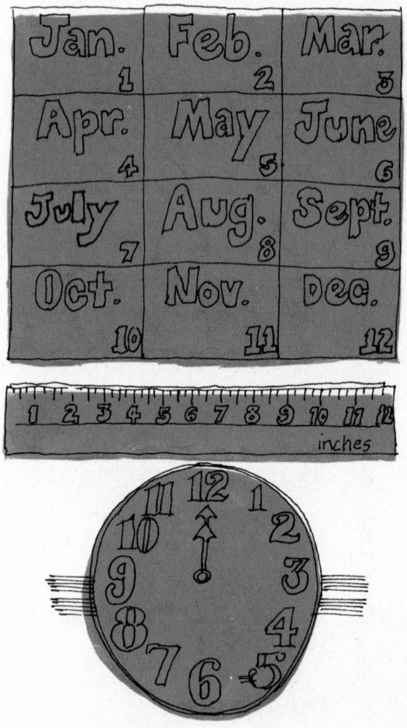

People have always had to measure things. They usually tried to set up a system that was easy to understand. The early measurements were made using the human body. Inches were measured by thumbs and fingers. Yards were measured by the length of an arm. Feet were measured by the length of a person's foot.

The number 12 became very important in measuring. A ruler that is a foot long has 12 inches (30 centimeters). A yardstick has 3 times 12 inches, or 36 inches (90 centimeters).

On a calendar, you will see 12 months in each year. A clock face is numbered from 1 to 12. Each day is 2 times 12, or 24 hours.

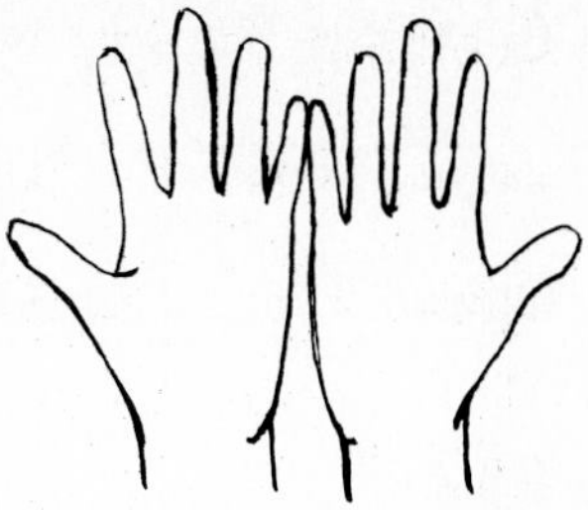

In the 1700s, a way of measuring called the *metric system* was set up. It was based on decimals, or on the number 10. Today the metric system is used more and more throughout the world. In 1975, President Gerald Ford signed a new law. The law said that the United States must change over to the metric system.

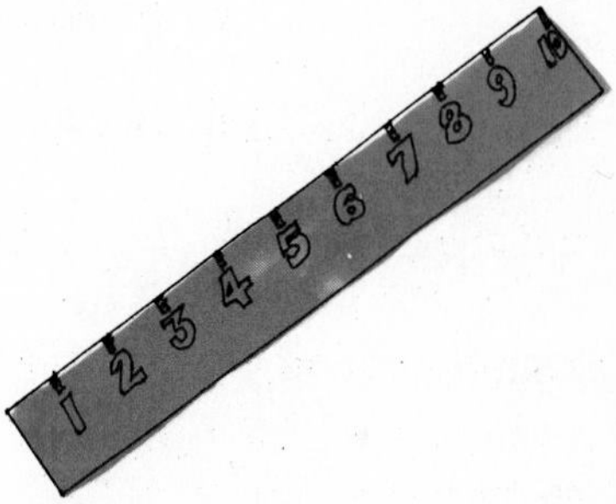

I-7 Testing Yourself

NUMBER RIGHT

Draw a line under the right answer or fill in the blank.

1. The metric system is based on ______________________.

2. From the story, you can tell that
  a. it is best if everyone uses the same measuring system.
  b. the number 6 is more important than the number 12.
  c. a yardstick measures 12 inches.

3. This story as a whole is about
  a. the ways people measure.
  b. buying things by the dozen.
  c. midnight shopping.
  d. measuring with a 12-inch ruler.

4. Sometimes we buy things by the half dozen. Yes No Does not say

5. Each year has 12 months. Yes No Does not say

6. What word in the fourth paragraph, second sentence, means **numbers based on 10?** ______________________

Getting Ready to Read

SAY AND KNOW

difficult
ashamed
parents
problems
neighborhoods
understand

Draw a line under the right answer or fill in the blank.

1. **Mothers and fathers** are **ashamed** **parents** **problems.**
2. It is **the opposite of feeling proud.** **ashamed** **problems** **difficult**
3. It means **hard to do.** **neighborhoods** **difficult** **understand**
4. **To know something** is to **be ashamed** **understand** **be difficult.**
5. **The area around you home** is your **neighborhood** **problem** **parents.**
6. **Difficult questions** are ______________.

I-8 In a New Land

In the late 1800s, many people left their countries for different reasons. They all hoped to find a better life in America.

One of the first problems they faced was work. In order to work, they had to speak English. They could do very well in their own neighborhoods. There, they spoke their own language. But on the job, they had to speak the new language.

Without English, they could not understand the rules and laws of their new country.

Even so, many of these people wanted to keep their own language and habits in their homes. Sometimes the language changes were a problem for their children. The young ones went to American schools. They had to learn the new ways. More and more, they became part of the American way of life. But often their parents did not. Sometimes the children were ashamed because their parents still dressed and talked as they had in the old country. The problems of learning to live happily in the new land were often difficult for these families to work out.

I-8 Testing Yourself

NUMBER RIGHT

Draw a line under the right answer or fill in the blank.

1. People who left their countries hoped to find a better ________.

2. From the story, you can tell that
- a. people were ready to work on their language problems.
- b. there weren't many problems with language.
- c. the new way of life caused problems within families.

3. This story as a whole is about
- a. the rules of working.
- b. children and parents.
- c. speaking English.
- d. language problems of immigrants.

4. Language was not a problem at all. Yes No Does not say

5. The schools made all the children write in English.
Yes No Does not say

6. What word in the last sentence means **not easy?** ________

Getting Ready to Read

SAY AND KNOW

poking

eardrum

concerned

noise pollution

crisscross

create

cause

Draw a line under the right answer or fill in the blank.

1. It means **to make happen.** **slap** **cause** **poke**
2. It is **part of the ear.** **eardrum** **concern** **crisscross**
3. **To be worried** is **to be** **concerned** **poked** **created.**
4. **Pushing or jabbing into something** means **creating** **causing** **poking.**
5. **Too much noise** is called **noise pollution** **eardrum** **crisscross.**
6. It means **to move back and forth and across.** ______________________

I-9 Guard Those Ears!

There are some things we can do to protect our ears. Loud noises too close to the ear may harm the eardrum. Because of this, we should not shout into another person's ear. Slapping the ear may harm the eardrum. Never hit anyone on the ear. Be careful, too, about poking sharp things into the ear.

People have been concerned about another cause of ear damage. They call the problem noise pollution. Our cities are busy places. Highways

crisscross in and out. Cars, buses, and huge trucks all add to the noise. When jet planes fly, they create loud noises. They, too, have added to the noise pollution.

People have come to realize that there are ways to deal with this problem. For example, workers who work with big machinery now wear earmuffs. This helps keep out the noise and helps protect the ears.

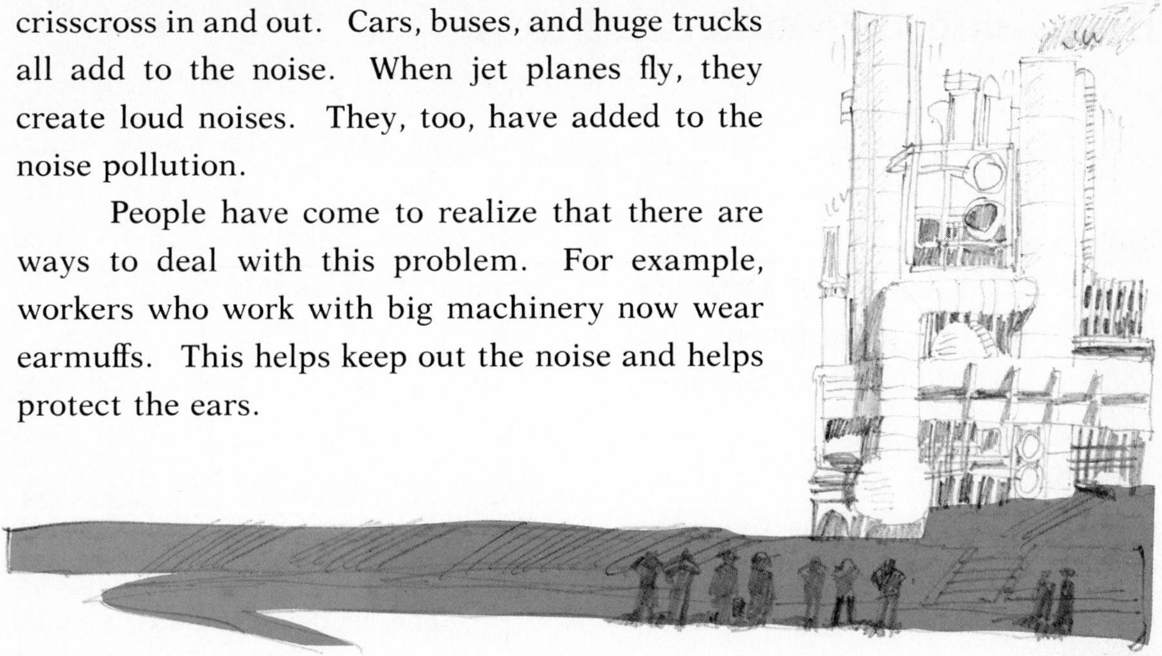

I-9 Testing Yourself

NUMBER RIGHT

Draw a line under the right answer or fill in the blank.

1. Loud noises may harm the ______________________.
2. From the story, you can tell that
   a. you should always wear earmuffs.
   b. some noise is always good.
   c. our ears can be easily hurt.
3. This story as a whole is about
   a. things that can harm our ears
   b. the middle ear.
   c. the eardrum.
   d. small problems in the ear.
4. Trucks don't cause noise pollution. Yes No Does not say
5. All ear problems are caused by the city. Yes No Does not say
6. What word in the last sentence means **keep from harm?**

____

Boone and the Wilderness Trail

Young Daniel Boone and his wife Rebeccah lived on a farm in North Carolina with their children. He had heard many tales about the wonderful rivers, deep forests, and wide plains that lay in the land beyond the mountains.

In May 1769, Boone and five others started on foot over the mountains toward Kentucky. They wore fringed hunting shirts, deerskin leggings, and moccasins. Each person carried a knife and a tomahawk. Each had a powder horn, a rifle, and a pouch of lead bullets. Explorers often had a Native American man or woman as a guide. But Boone and his group traveled alone. They followed an old explorers trail called the Warrior's Path. Travel along the path was slow and difficult. Finally, after five weeks, they reached the top of the mountains. They looked down upon a beautiful land.

The six friends built a small cabin near a river. For months they hunted and explored, sometimes going farther and farther west. They had many exciting adventures.

One day, while they were crossing an open plain, they came on a great buffalo herd. The animals raced toward the hunters. There seemed to be no escape. But one man knew the ways of these animals. He shot and killed one of the lead bulls, then told his friends to stand behind the dead animal. The herd divided and went around its fallen leader. The men were saved.

Another time, when Boone and one friend were hunting far from their cabin, they were held by Native Americans. Boone showed great patience and courage. He was friendly to the tribe. Finally, he and his friend were let go without harm. When they returned to their cabin, everything was in disorder. Their four friends had disappeared. These men were never seen again.

Boone and his companion stayed on, trapping for beavers and other animals. Soon Boone's brother joined them. Then the last friend also disappeared. The brothers became very careful. In May, Boone's brother started for home. His horses were loaded with furs. He returned safely in July. He brought good news of the Boone family in North Carolina.

In 1775, Boone led a group into Kentucky. Their job was to improve the old trails that led into the new land. They were to join these trails to one another. The route that Boone and the others made became the famous Wilderness Road. This path was used by many pioneers traveling into the new lands. It was on this trip that

Boone began the construction of a fort called Boonesborough.

Many more exciting tales are told of Daniel Boone's adventures in Kentucky. Once there was danger on three sides of him. On the fourth side was a high river bank. Boone leaped over the bank and landed in the top of a big tree. He quickly slid down the tree and ran along the river bank. Then he jumped into the river, swam across, and escaped.

Boone claimed much land in the Kentucky Territory for his own. But because of changes in land laws, he lost everything he thought was his. By 1798, the famous woodsman was again moving west to make his fortune. He went to Missouri, which at that time was a Spanish territory. Boone lived happily in the new country. He continued to roam and hunt in the wilderness until he died at the age of eighty-six.

MY READING TIME ______ (458 WORDS)

Thinking It Over

1. What might have been happening with Rebeccah and the family during these years?
2. How did the Native Americans feel about outsiders coming into their land?
3. What skills did Boone need to live in the wilderness?

Keeping Track of Growth

Diagnostic Progress Records

Study this sample graph. To record the score for Unit A, put a dot on the line beside the number which tells how often Question 4 was answered correctly. Do the same for Units B, C, and so on. Draw a line to join the dots. The line will show how this reading skill is growing.

Notice that each graph records the progress made on one question. See how this reader improved in answering Question 4 in each unit except Unit E.

Sample

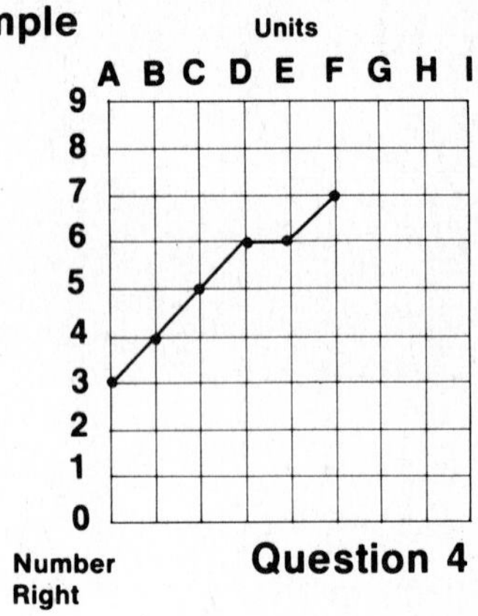

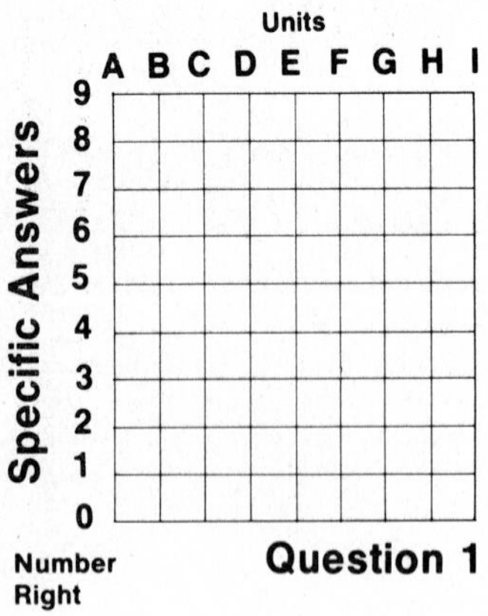

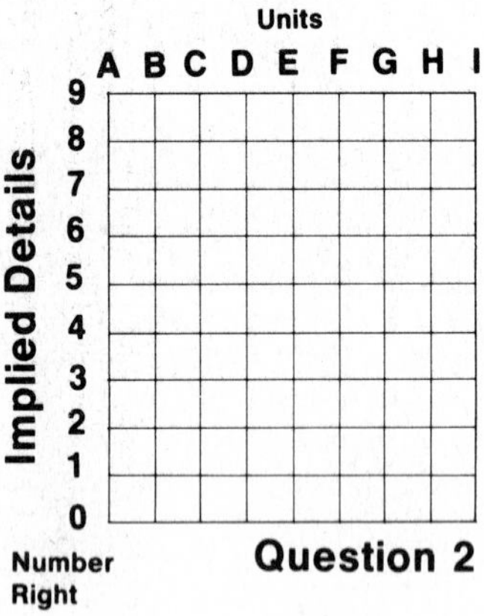

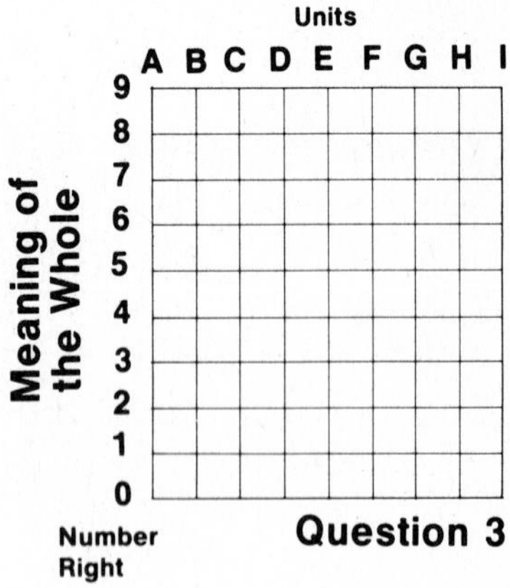

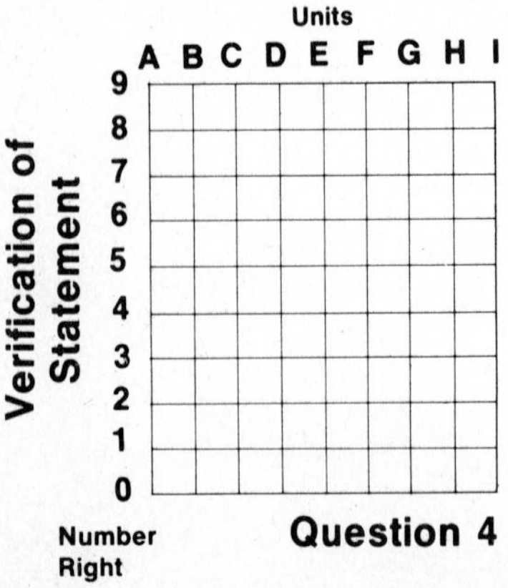

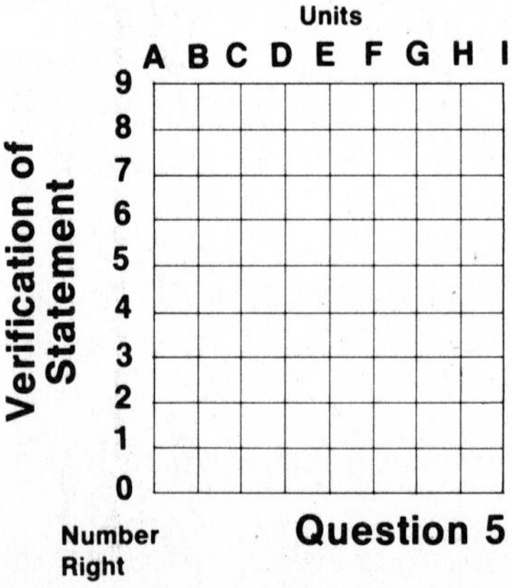

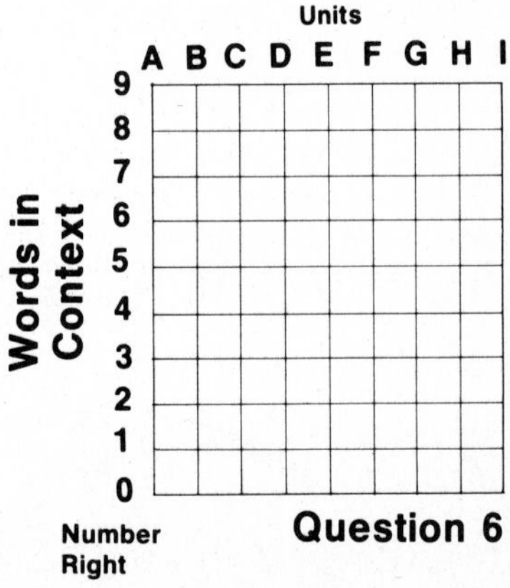